To my family, who has supported

me through all of my pursuits.

The Pre-Med Survival Guide

Copyright ©2015 by Tyler L. Scaff

thepremedsurvivalguide@gmail.com

ISBN # 978-1512027921

Printed in the United States of America by Createspace™

CreateSpace™ is a DBA of On-Demand Publishing LLC, part of the Amazon group of companies.

The Pre-Med Survival Guide

A Complete Guide to College for
the Future Physician

Tyler L. Scaff

With Foreword by Luke C. Murray, M.D.

Table of Contents

Foreword

In the summer of 2014 I was asked to give a talk to the Professional Education Preparation Program (PEPP) group at the University of Kentucky. These students are among the sharpest and most ambitious in the state and know that they want to end up in a graduate school in one of the health professions - usually medical school. The title of the talk was "What I Wish I'd Known as a Pre-Med" and at the end of it, I mentioned that I was writing a book for medical students about navigating the emotionally difficult time that is (usually) your mid-20's while simultaneously tackling the intellectually and professionally difficult time that is medical school.

Tyler approached me and mentioned that he, too, was writing a book. His was a guide specifically for pre-meds. He asked if he could keep in touch and send me updates and I gladly agreed, expecting never to hear from him again, as was the most common result from conversations with aspiring authors.

But every few weeks I got an update on his progress. Questions about publishing. Pieces of writing. Until finally I received, read through, and edited a full manuscript - an accomplishment that few people I've ever spoken to have achieved.

When he asked me to write this foreword, I felt compelled to address the same audience he did, for the same reasons he did: the version of myself that was about to begin college as a pre-med student, in order to prevent him from making the same mistakes I did.

While the pre-med version of Luke existed 14 years ago, reading Tyler's book helped refresh my memory about the things I did right, reminded me of the things I did wrong, and opened my mind up to things I hadn't even considered. You're about to read what someone who has just finished the pre-med process has to say about things he wish he'd known. On a journey that usually lasts at least a dozen years, he can tell you how to live the first four.

Here's what someone who's got just 12 months left before being finished, has to say about those same four years.

Hey mid-college Luke, it's me. The 32 year old version of you. I know you're super excited about becoming a brain surgeon at the moment and it's great that you've reached out to all the neurosurgeons at UK, and I want you to have high goals.

But please. Calm down and do less.

When you are my age, you're going to look back on this time of your life and think, "I could have had a lot more fun, been a lot less stressed and still accomplished my goals if I would have just done a few things differently, like...

"...Paid attention to what works and what doesn't, and had the courage to make the changes necessary to apply this knowledge."

Remember when you made that list of goals at the end of your first semester and by the end of your second semester had accomplished none of them? Why did you keep making an equally long and ambitious list every year? How many times did you try to study in your dorm room and get distracted, and a planned 3-hour study session turned into a session of "Fat Man's Volleyball" in the lobby? You were only behind and staying up late at night because you didn't admit that it's worth the ten or twenty minutes necessary to go find a hiding place where you can't be interrupted or distracted to ensure that you actually get a good two hours of studying in. And *then* you can do the butt-puckering experiment of *"launch-water-balloon-straight-into-night-sky-with-massive-slingshot-and-whoever-runs-for-cover-first-loses,"* guilt free.

"...Done less." You're going to have plenty of extra-curricular activities to put on your AMCAS. Don't worry about taking **every** opportunity to pad your résumé that comes your way. Plus, you're late for everything, can't give your all to anything, and are really missing out on developing relationships and making an impact on the things you really care about. Which brings me to my next point…

"...Done what I liked." You're doing a good job creating your own major (combining business and medicine), but what do you really want to learn? What would you like to know? And what things outside of the classroom really make you happy? Get crystal clear on this because you're more likely to use that knowledge (and end up in a field that needs it) and be happier than if you didn't.

"...Relaxed." You're going to look back on this time and see a lot of missed fun. Why? Not because you had chosen a path that is inevitably filled with misery, but because you didn't do those first three things. If you were studying more efficiently, doing a few things instead of a million and making sure that you enjoyed the few activities you were doing, you could relax knowing you were on the right track...especially if you were *also* reading things like *"The Pre-Med Survival Guide"*.

Luke C. Murray, M.D.
Second Year Resident, Family Medicine
University of Kentucky

Introduction

Medicine is a calling.

Those of us who wish to dedicate our lives to the well-being of others practice perhaps the most intimate ministry there is: we are entrusted with the private struggles of our fellow men and women for the purpose of mitigating their suffering. There is, in my opinion, no higher cause than to heal the sick and care for the healthy.

The field of medicine spans countless jobs, from the orderly to the administrator, but few of these are as difficult to attain as the physician. Being the voice of authority on all things medical, the physician is entrusted with the greatest responsibilities of any healthcare professional; as such, they have the most rigorous process of schooling.

If you, like me, also desire to pursue this immensely rewarding career track, then I congratulate you on your desire to join the medical family. However, it is very important that you first familiarize yourself with the challenges that await you prior to choosing the path of the doctor.

In order to become a physician, you must undergo formal schooling for a minimum of eleven years after high school: four years of college, four years of medical school, a one-year internship, and at least two years of residency in your specialty of choice. It is important to realize that you will not start making any money at all until your internship and residency (eight years after graduating high school), at which time you will be paid approximately $40,000 per year until your residency is complete.

Speaking of money, doctors are saddled with far more debt than they used to be. While the median physician's salary in 2013 was still high at $268,000[1], it is common knowledge that today's medical student graduates with over $150,000 in debt. Moreover, the practice of medicine has lost some of its prestige with the advent of the internet, which patients may use to self-diagnose, and the postmillennial upswing in lawsuit popularity, which has forced physicians to spend a significant portion of their money on malpractice insurance. Doctors are also becoming more administrative: the majority spend less than sixteen minutes in the room with each patient, and between five and fourteen *hours* per week filling out paperwork[1]. All in all, if today's doctors had to do it over again, nineteen percent report that they would pick their same practice setting (hospital, clinic, and so forth), forty-two percent would pick their same *specialty*, and just fifty-one percent[1] would choose medicine as a career to begin with!

The difficulties of medical school are well-known; "drinking water from a firehose" is how some medical students describe a day's worth of lecture material. Most people who are interested in the physician's career path, however, are so focused on medical school that they ignore the four years that come *before* medical school. These four years are the first proving ground of the aspiring physician.

In order to be a medical student, you must first learn *how* to be a medical student. This means taking four years of college courses in the most difficult and esoteric scientific concepts offered to undergraduates (that is, college students who do not already have a Bachelor's degree). Contrary to

---

[1] Medscape Physician Compensation Report: 2013. (2013). Retrieved March 16, 2015.

popular belief, the purpose of these courses is *not* to teach you material relevant to medicine! The primary objective of the pre-med curriculum is instead to put you through a mental "boot camp", where you grow used to performing under pressure and learning difficult concepts quickly.

Successful completion of the pre-med curriculum is determined by your Grade Point Average (GPA) and a satisfactory score on the Medical College Admission Test (MCAT); these two numbers tell medical schools how well you could absorb their medical curriculum and thus, in theory, how knowledgeable of a doctor you could become. Combined with your résumé of activities performed while in college, admissions committees will be able to synthesize an image of you as a medical student, evaluate your capability for success, and make their decision accordingly.

My name is Tyler Scaff, and I am a pre-med at Western Kentucky University. Having spent six years in college, I am graduating WKU and matriculating to the University Of Kentucky College Of Medicine in the fall of this year. I leave this university with a great deal of appreciation for the struggles that must be weathered by the aspiring physician, and a detailed knowledge of how to navigate the obstacles you are now facing or will soon encounter. My goal in writing this book is to provide you with an honest and thorough resource to navigate most of the challenges that await you during the first four years of your long road. Whether you are a first-generation college student or from a long line of successful medical professionals, there is something you can learn from this book. I will show you the professional, personal, and academic obstacles I and my fellow successful graduates faced, and how we overcame them.

First, however, I will spend two chapters asking you to analyze your commitment to this career path, which must be absolute and unshakable if you are to conquer the hard road ahead. As you read this book, remember the maxim that is true for all of the difficult paths in life, and certainly for the path of the pre-med: if it were easy, everyone would do it.

Good luck.

About Me

Before I got my acceptance to medical school, I wanted to know everything there was to know about the pre-med students in the classes ahead of me who were accepted, from what they got on their MCAT to what they had for breakfast. Now that I have been accepted, I have received numerous requests from sophomores and juniors wanting to know what *I* have for breakfast. And so, the cycle continues.

These requests were one of the catalysts for writing this book; I already feel that I have written reams of advice to my inquisitive and intelligent successors. Indeed, many of the passages you find in this book were adapted from advice I gave over social media and email. I am not keen on taking advice from people who I do not feel are qualified to give it, however, and I imagine you are the same way. In this chapter, I hope to show you that I am qualified to give you advice on being a pre-med in college. My mistakes and successes both have taught me lessons from which you can learn. Like my father said to me: you choose the road, and I can fill in some of the potholes.

Kindling interest

The little me started in San Diego, California, where I lived until I was eight years old. During that time, I showed interest in science, but not specifically in medicine. I was tended to by the best family physician I have ever known, and whose bedside manner I aim to emulate. He was honest, soothing, and made sure that his hands and stethoscope were clean and warm before using them on anyone. His dedication to his patients was unquestionable; my father would receive calls from him regarding his prescriptions while this physician was eating lunch. Finally, he knew how to manage every aspect of his practice from the clerk's desk to the exam room. My father distinctly recalls seeing him pull files from the nurse's station as if he had done it all his life. In all of those ways, I aim to be like that doctor.

When we moved to Kentucky, I was just entering third grade. There I went to school in Oldham County and attended a little stone church on the corner. It was in Kentucky that my interest in science first began to develop; my interest in medicine specifically would come later.

The first change I noticed in Kentucky schools was the fact that I had to do homework for the first time in my life. California's elementary schools only recommended homework, but that did not fly in Kentucky. Over time, and with several disciplinary actions against me, I developed an appreciation for hard work. My parents did not pay me or in any way reward me for my grades; they were my own, and the only person I had to answer to was me. Strangely enough, that motivated me to do well even more than money could have, though at the time I found it to be unfair.

I can't say for sure what first piqued my interest in medicine; maybe it was Flick from *A Bug's Life* saying "I just want to help." That quote stuck with me, and I realized that my main desire in life was to help other people. I have always had a deep sense of empathy for my fellow man; it hurts me to see someone, anyone, in pain. Whether it was a cartoon character who was shot out of a cannon, or a kid who bruised his knee on the playground, I was absolutely not okay with it. I didn't care if I hated the kid or the cartoon character was evil; I did not want to see them get hurt. Later in life, this empathy would work against some beliefs and hobbies that I had chosen to pursue.

I began to develop a strong humanist side in my freshman year of high school, despite being something of a bully in middle school. Since I was often the stereotypical last kid to be picked for a sports team, being the "nerd", I developed a sense of kinship with my fellow misfits who lost every flag football and dodgeball game they played. I find that even today, I root for the little guy. Whenever I win at a competition against another person, be it a strategy game or a bagpiping tournament, I feel a little sense of sadness knowing that someone else lost. It is usually only a small twinge at the back of my mind, since I am a very competitive person and love to win, but nonetheless I have never been able to detach myself from their pain of losing, no matter how good it feels when I win.

At this point, I should probably address the peculiar fact that I spent my younger years as a butt-kicking bagpiper. My parents enrolled me and my sister in martial arts from an early age, rather than having us join the school sports teams. Their reasoning was that martial arts teaches you valuable life skills, reflex action, limb-eye coordination, and mental acuity. While true, it is also worth noting that martial arts is not really a team sport, so we only learned to work as part of a team much later in life. I personally chose to follow my father's footsteps and become a player of the Highland Bagpipes, which I still play today. My passion for music is only surpassed by my passion for medicine, and playing such a unique instrument allowed me to bond with a small community of very interesting people. However, it also made certain that I would be known as the "bagpipe guy" in high school...not exactly the reputation I had in mind. I suppose it could have been worse.

Though I kept on piping, I decided to pursue other methods of exercise after I realized that I enjoyed swimming, crossfit, hiking, caving, and other physically challenging activities that did not require me to hit people. Though I did enjoy the mentality of martial arts, I did not enjoy causing others pain, even if it was just a sport. Still, martial arts did teach me a great deal about self-discipline and self-defense, and it was an excellent thing to do while growing up.

Building the foundation

High school was…interesting. I spent my first two years at a public school in Oldham County and my latter two enrolled in the fledgling Carol Martin Gatton Academy at Western Kentucky University (Gatton for short). The contrast between the two was remarkable: Gatton forced me to study, pushed me to my academic limits, and showed me how far I could really go. In many ways, it was exactly how I imagine medical school will be: small classes, immense workloads, and a strong support system designed not only to keep you going, but to actually *enjoy* what you're doing.

Over those last two years of high school, I finally learned the lesson that my parents had been trying to teach me: life is so much better when you push yourself to the limit. When you strike out in new directions, take courses in topics you are only cursorily familiar with, exercise until you can't breathe, try new things precisely because they terrify you, and shoot for the highest star you can reach, that lifestyle will build precisely the person you have always wanted to be. It is in the hottest forge that the best steel is made. I started Gatton not knowing if I could even handle the workload, and I graduated Summa cum Laude with a 3.96 GPA.

My time in Gatton also afforded me a chance to explore my faith, which culminated in my decision to depart with Christianity. I could not reconcile my humanist personality with the idea of Hell; I asked myself what I would do if, on Judgment Day, I was told by God that I was allowed into Heaven, but my mother, or friend, or even someone I did not know at all was sentenced to eternal torment for reasons I viewed to be unjust. My answer to that question led me to the realization that I constantly was putting humans above God, and therefore violating the Ten Commandments. Rather than disrespect the faith by lying to others (and myself), I chose to leave the faith under good terms. I have great respect for Christians, and for religion in general, but I realized over the course of Gatton that I am not a member of that faith. It's a lonely road when you give up a community like that, but I know I made the right decision. Now, I do not identify with any specific perspective, and am comfortable with exploring the questions of the beyond for myself.

Folly of arrogance

After graduating Gatton, my head was as big as it could have gotten. For college, I chose to go to the University of North Carolina at Chapel Hill, a university that, while offering a marginally higher academic reputation than WKU (which was the basis of my decision), did not offer me one cent of a scholarship. Then the real workload started; all of a sudden I was thrust into a world where the support system I had enjoyed in Gatton was all but nonexistent.

Being an out-of-state student is a nightmare if you do not know anyone at the university. It's lonely to know that your loved ones are hundreds of miles away. Even the social groups that all freshmen have did not work for me; I mostly met people who I thought were a chore to be around. Combined with the fluorescent hellhole of a freshman dorm, a roommate who acted like he owned the room, and a difficult relationship, life was rough, and it got harder when I decided not to pursue medicine.

I mentioned before that I had an interest in becoming a doctor since I was young. I distinctly recall sitting in sixth grade math class and deciding to myself that I was going to attend the University of Kentucky for medical school. (It was not because of the school, but rather because they had a really cool wildcat as a mascot.) As I got older, I realized I had not really taken the time when I was younger to explore other careers. Having interests in many fields, I could probably have chosen to become one of several different things and been reasonably happy. This lack of informedness about what else was out there prompted me to pursue other careers in my freshman year of college. I told myself that if the introductory biology courses I took were the bread-and-butter for medicine (e.g. cells, evolution, and the suffocating science of genetics), then I wanted nothing to do with it.

After that decision, I explored many different careers, from mathematician to computer scientist to HH-60 pilot in the Air Force. I did not find a single one that fit me well enough, other than being an astronaut. I am already an astro-nut, and I enjoy the science and challenge of the job, but it's not really practical to shoot for that field directly given how few people get the opportunity to go to space. It was a very scary feeling not to know what career to focus on, and even after taking all those personality tests and a course devoted to career exploration, I still was not sure what I wanted to do. Time was running out.

In a last-ditch attempt to find something that interested me, I asked my elementary school teachers, and my parents, what I was interested in when I was young. Somehow, I had become so lost in the limitless opportunities of college that I had forgotten what I had wanted since I was young. As you can imagine, the response was, "Are you kidding? You have always wanted to be a doctor." (And astronaut.)

Before this information clicked into place, however, more immediate concerns at UNC interrupted my career exploration.

Request to transfer

At UNC, I was on a significant amount of financial aid from the government. However, when my freshman year ended, my estimated family contribution (the part of financial aid applications where the government decides what your family should pay) shot through the roof. The government has a two-page-long equation that they use to calculate your EFC, and that equation had decided that since my sister graduated from her college, we would have more free money to pay for my college. The trouble with that reasoning was that my sister was on a full-ride scholarship, and her graduation did not affect our family financially in the least. It was my responsibility to know the details of my financial aid, but I thought too highly of myself to think that my university would not bend over backwards for me. That arrogance deprived me of my savings, put me in debt, and almost cost me my college career. However, Western Kentucky University allowed me to transfer back.

When I returned home, I went to a routine appointment with the dentist I had had since we moved to Kentucky. I had not seen her in a while, so she did not know of my decision to explore careers other than medicine. We talked for a while, with me attempting to make conversation while my mouth was full of tools.

She asked me how my pre-med progress was going, and I attempted to tell her (how do dentists expect their patients to talk to them like this?) that I was pursuing computer science now, and I had turned away from medicine. Then, the funniest twist of fate happened: she didn't hear me. She just went right on giving me advice about programs to get involved with when I returned to school in the fall. Later I learned that she just had not understood what I had said with a mouth full of tools, but at the time I thought she had pretended not to hear me. It appeared to me that she thought my desire to do anything but medicine was just a ridiculous passing fancy, not even worth discussing. For once, my habit of reading too much into situations worked out in my favor.

I began to ask myself, *what the hell am I doing?* Why had I given up on something that I had wanted since I was a kid? So, not entirely convinced, I registered at the last minute for a WKU course in general chemistry, a required pre-med course, and set up some dates for shadowing. After spending time in that class and cramming myself into tiny exam rooms, I would realize that being a physician was what I had wanted to do all along.

Returning home

My financial naïveté about college shattered, I began to re-integrate into the university which I once thought myself to be above. Life was excruciating; I can personally attest to the power that financial worry has over your psyche. I had the bitter realization that my parents were paying for my time at WKU, since I was not offered much of a scholarship as a transfer student. I had planned since high school to earn a full ride to a university so my parents wouldn't have to pay a cent on my path to medicine, but my arrogance ensured that would not come to pass. Guilt, combined with teenage angst, made it difficult to control my emotions. As a result, my first two years of college were to be the most miserable of my life.

To make things worse, I enrolled myself in volunteer opportunities, job opportunities, and research opportunities that, while I hated them, looked very flashy on my résumé. I did not believe there would ever be extracurricular activities that were both enjoyable and good-looking, so I did everything from volunteer firefighting to working in bioinformatics research. I also did extensive shadowing, which was about the only thing I did enjoy.

When I first started shadowing, I expected doctors to tell me all about how they were class president in their high school, held offices in five different clubs in college, did research, studied their asses off, and had absolutely no social life (you may perhaps expect the same). That is why it floored me to learn that every physician I shadowed lived the life of a somewhat normal college student. They pursued personal projects, drank and partied, buckled down when they needed to, but most of all, lived. It was the overstressed workaholics that eventually left the profession or lost momentum because the misery of their work just became too much for them.

As I thought about it more, I began to wonder if I had been approaching this pre-med thing the complete wrong way. What if you do not, and should not, have to be miserable on the road to medicine? Follow me on this train of thought: First, you have to get into college. Next, you have to do well on the MCAT. Next, you have to get into medical school. Then, you have to do well on medical school exams like Step 1 and Step 2. Then, you have to get into a residency. Then, you have to get into a fellowship. Finally, you have to be a physician, which is far and away one of the most difficult jobs that exists! When, I asked myself, have I "made it"? When can I start living my life instead of the one that goes on my applications?

I answered that question as I answered the perennial question of why I want to be a doctor: because it's just who I am as a person. The reason I did not allow myself to drop out of college after the issues I had in freshman year was because I was working towards a career in medicine, and that drove me more than anything else. Medical schools did not want me to focus my life around what I thought the perfect pre-med would do. Had I done that, I may well have dropped the whole idea long ago. I was already someone who would make a great doctor; I just had to show it by doing things *I* was passionate about.

Hitting my stride

In my junior year, things changed. I dropped the obligations I did not enjoy and started taking ones I did. I found that I really enjoyed student government, and so I got involved with that. I enjoyed shadowing, so I did more of that. I enjoyed volunteering at a camp where I led kids with disabilities around on horses, so I did that too. My life immediately began to improve; even when I was studying for the Medical College Admission Test (MCAT), I was neither overworked nor unhappy.

I will tell you all about how I studied for the MCAT in a later chapter, since I know when I was in your shoes I wanted to know everything I could. Here is a brief synopsis: I registered to take the exam on May 22nd, 2014, from 8:00 AM to 1:00 PM, and I booked that date the fall beforehand. My reasoning was that I would give myself an entire semester to study, and May 22nd was the Thursday after finals week. Any later than that, I thought, and I would be in "summer mode" (i.e., too lazy to study).

After registering, I spent the remainder of my fall semester familiarizing myself with the components of the MCAT. I read the official online resources from the Association of American of Medical Colleges (AAMC), including the comprehensive list of every topic they could ask me about. Then, I worked through free familiarization materials available from test prep companies like Kaplan. By the time I finished the fall semester of 2013, I knew the anatomy of the MCAT and what topics I would have to study.

Over the winter break, I got $40 worth of older Kaplan study books and signed up for the $200 MCAT Prep

Course offered at WKU. I purchased the official MCAT study guide from AAMC, and first began looking at that in late January. However, most of my winter break was spent resting.

I also began to trim the fat in my schedule: with only twelve hours of coursework, three of which were biochemistry, I was prepared to spend the majority of each day of the week studying for the test. I dropped some extracurricular obligations, quit my job at the local planetarium, and instead took a job as a physics tutor, which was by far the best thing I could have done for my study habits. Not only did the job reinforce concepts that were tested on the MCAT, it also put me in a quiet workplace for three days out of the week. When a student came in, I got to study physics. When no one came in, I pulled out the old Kaplan books and read chapters in detail. It was the ideal job for an MCAT student, better than having no job at all.

My study schedule outside of work was designed to force me to study intensively for hours at a time, right around the time of day that I would be taking the test. In the morning, I adopted a strict morning routine: Up at six, with a bowl of oatmeal and black coffee, and a couple of cartoon episodes. I started studying or working at eight in the morning each day, except for Sunday. On Saturdays, I had the MCAT prep class which lasted for an average of four hours. In those classes, we covered a lot of lecture and took a total of twelve official AAMC practice tests.

The practice tests, which I only took directly from AAMC, were the most helpful parts of studying. Not only did I get familiar with taking the test itself, but I also developed a routine for the breaks (one granola bar and half an energy shot) and conditioned my brain to survive long hours of testing. Since I had not purchased a Kaplan course or the like, I only had access to the AAMC's practice tests, and that was probably a good thing. I was (and still am) of the opinion that the only company capable of giving you a reasonably accurate practice MCAT is the company which administers the real MCAT.

In retrospect, I was the most prepared to take the MCAT in March, and I was actually *less* prepared for the test in May. When you study such immense amounts of material, some is bound to get lost. By the time the MCAT rolled around, that which I studied in February was awfully foggy. This is why I never advise students to study for the recommended three hundred hours; you will just forget what you learned in the first hundred. I studied for a total of two hundred or so, but was most prepared after just one hundred. It also did not help that after finals week, I was too burnt out from the semester to stay focused for another week.

Studying for the MCAT is not like studying for any other test; you can't just cram all the knowledge into your brain and expect it to stay there. Much like medical school, there is just too much for one person to know, and so you must prioritize your studying. After taking a "benchmark" practice MCAT, the AAMC's feedback software told me which topics I needed to study the most. I studied those and barely touched the rest; instead of pushing for perfect knowledge of just a few fields like embryology or harmonic motion, I developed a working understanding of most of the topics. That way, when the MCAT finally came, I was reasonably prepared no matter what they chose to test me on.

The old MCAT was scored out of forty-five points, with the average for matriculating medical students sitting somewhere around thirty. I got a 32. This score, while definitely satisfying for me, was not the highest score I had received on my practice tests; my highest was actually a 36, and I received that over spring break in March. To explain why this happened, it is important to point out that the more you take practice tests, the more you will establish your bell curve of possible scores. Your lowest score could be a seventeen, and your highest a thirty-seven, but often you will earn somewhere close to a thirty-three. That, then, would be the score you are likely to get when you take the real MCAT.

Under the spotlight

In March of that semester, the AAMC's universal medical school application opened; this was the document that would later be sent to all the medical schools to which I applied. I began filling out the application the day it opened, and when the submission window opened a month later, I submitted it immediately. I knocked on doors and sent many emails to ensure that all my required application components were delivered on-time; indeed, the only thing that really delayed my application was the MCAT score report. After taking the test, you are given one month to chew your nails before your score arrives, so it was not until I was in the thick of summer that I received news of my score. With a 32 MCAT and a 3.84 GPA, though, I was in a good situation.

After that, I filled out secondary applications for those medical schools that sent me them, paid some more money, and had them all taken care of before my senior year began in August. My reasoning for getting the secondaries done so quickly, apart from getting first dibs on interview invitations, was that I may not have time to devote to filling out the applications when school kicked back into gear. Fortunately, I received my first interview request in August, and interviewed shortly after that. This was at the University of Louisville, and I also interviewed at the University of Kentucky in September. I did receive secondaries from Johns Hopkins, Duke, and Wake Forest, but no interview invitations. I did not receive a secondary from Vanderbilt.\

After receiving my first acceptance on October 16th of that year, I was both relieved and relaxed. However, I did not get senioritis until the spring semester; in fact, the fall semester of my senior year was spent founding a club, volunteering, and being a committee chair of student government! It was amazing; when I no longer felt the need to prove myself to medical schools, I actually was *more* productive. I also performed better in class than I ever had before!

Looking back

That brings me to today, where I am ready to graduate college and begin medical school in late July. Out of the two schools to which I was accepted, I have decided to attend the University of Kentucky College Of Medicine. Their impressive financial aid system (and the fact that I can apply for loans as an independent) has ensured that I will have support for the entirety of medical school. I am a very happy camper.

College was a time of immense personal growth for me; I went from self-loathing and insecure to a leader of the community in a comparably small amount of time, though it felt like ages when I was going through the hard transformations. I left a lot of my childhood ways behind, and today, I have an open mind and a bright perspective. Four more years of formal schooling await me and I cannot wait to get started.

I still have not forgotten about my dreams of ultimately becoming an astronaut, but in order to even apply for the program you have to have a doctorate in something, including medicine. So, I realized that the best route for me was to become a physician and then apply for NASA when in my residency. Today, and every day, I hold to that plan.

Though I experienced the roughest time of my life in college, I would not be the person I am today without facing those challenges. The period of my life that forced me to question my convictions to medicine ultimately reinforced them; it made them unbreakable. I have seen what else life has to offer me, and with that information, I have chosen to be a doctor knowing that there is nothing else on this earth that is more important to me. Well, except maybe what is above it.

Reasons Not to Be a Pre-Med

Because of my time at the Carol Martin Gatton Academy at Western Kentucky University, I ended up spending six years in undergraduate college (five at WKU, one at the University of North Carolina at Chapel Hill). At Gatton, I was a pre-med; at UNC, I majored in computer science; when I returned to WKU, I became a pre-med again. I've spent a long time among students of every major, and out of all of them, the pre-med undergoes perhaps the most radical personal transformations while in college.

In their freshman year, a budding pre-med is much like any other new college student in that they are inevitably awed by the wonderful array of freedoms they now enjoy. Away from their parents, college students can go out with friends any time of the day or night. They are free to plan their own class schedule, keep their room as messy as they want it, eat to their heart's content, and generally make their own decisions for the first time. Many will take this year to explore new pastimes, different religious beliefs, or even their own sexuality. In this new environment, a freshman can expect to undergo many personal changes over the next four years as they slowly become the person they want to be.

Unfortunately, the freedom of college comes with an equal measure of responsibility, especially for the pre-med. As sophomore year dawns, pre-meds often find themselves slammed with the realities of their chosen profession. Suddenly, intimidating acronyms like "MCAT", "AMCAS", and "AACOMAS" are being thrown around. Classes kick into high gear, and pre-meds for the first time feel themselves under the watchful eye of medical school application committees. It is in this year that the pre-med's dedication to becoming a doctor is first tested.

But it gets worse. If this sophomore wants a glimpse of their junior and senior year, they should take the elevator a few floors up to the Biochemistry class. Up there, a small group of frazzled men and women are getting carpal tunnel from taking notes from their professor who talks like an auctioneer. The pre-med would observe a fashion style that obeys the "Smell Test" rule (if it smells alright, put it on) and no other, disposable coffee cups decorating tiny desks, bloodshot eyes, grinding teeth, and a palpable atmosphere of stress. This pre-med may never have seen these people before, because their only pastime consists of wolfing down a cold sandwich as they powerwalk to their next class, seminar, meeting, or extra-credit brownnosing opportunity. Such upperclassmen enjoy long hours of studying, a shot of vodka (it's medicinal), slaving over their résumé, thinking about giving up, and going to the bathroom in the middle of lecture, not because they had to go, but rather to avoid screaming in frustration at the professor.

The truths in this chapter are accurate enough to hurt. I would encourage you to read this chapter very carefully, as the best way to make the decision to be a pre-med is to throw yourself in the opposite direction; to allow me and others to give you every legitimate reason *not* to pursue medicine. If these facts fail to sway you from the path, then you'll know what you truly want to do with your life.

"You're a pre-med? So what?"

First, few people will ever care that you're a pre-med. To many professors, you're a pair of cheap hands under their command. If they want you to be a tech in their lab (i.e. fill out paperwork and refill chemicals), you do it. For free. If they want you to be a TA in their class, you thank them for the opportunity, and you don't ask for a check. Some have no qualms about singling you out in class, be it for a compliment or an accusation, and you'd better smile and thank them either way. They will slam you with their political and religious views left and right, and even if you disagree, you had better agree with them. They will rarely be merciful, and they will rarely be understanding. The only rules they have to follow are the ones they write in their syllabus.

To other college students, particularly those not in the sciences, the fact that you're a pre-med may raise an eyebrow in conversation. That's about it. Fact of the matter is, other college students are too wrapped up in their own lives to care about yours, and this is especially true for those in tough majors like physics, engineering, music, or computer science. Starting in your sophomore year, you will begin to feel indignant when you overhear an art history major complaining about their "Intro to Biology" class. Compared to you, most everyone else has it easy.

The stress gets worse

When I shadowed in an ER on New Year's Eve, I met a grizzled doctor who was just leaving for home after working the night shift. After the physician I was following introduced me to him and said that I also wanted to become a physician, the man grunted, "Be smart. Play one on TV."

Too many pre-meds seem to feel that being a doctor is easier than being a medical student, or even a pre-med! Nothing could be further from the truth. If you want to know how stressful a job in medicine really is, I would encourage you to ask the doctors you shadow. Like me, you will hear horror stories that will make you question your choice of career. Nightmares such as malpractice lawsuits, belligerent patients, and invasive family members are frequent visitors to the world of medicine, and I advise you to find out what being a doctor is really like before you decide to go for it.

Thankless studying

A fundamental truth about the pre-medical curriculum is that it will always get harder, not easier. Failure will be less and less tolerated as you proceed through college, to the point that a low grade in a senior-level class may preclude you from admission to medical school. Your responsibilities will continue to balloon throughout college as your social circle and "free time" atrophy. It is possible that you will miss out on a lot of the experiences that a "normal" college student has simply because you are too busy, and friends may not be understanding of your stress. All in all, being a pre-med is a thankless and hard row to hoe.

No medical training

As a pre-med, I have often been asked by family members and friends to look into "little problems" they've been having for "a while" and see what I can do. My response to them is always something similar to this: "I could tell you all about how to change the boiling point of liquid titanium, or how a circuit works, but I would have no idea where to begin with your problem." We laugh it off, of course, but the fact remains that for the next four years, you will be learning about everything you don't need to know. You may take a handful of organic chemistry, biochemistry, and anatomy to medical school (all of which are classes you typically get in your junior or senior year), but most of your time will be spent learning about the history of Europe, the geography of the Middle East, extracting caffeine from tea, the anatomy of a starfish, and how to find X. To get your medical fix, you will have to pester doctors to get some shadowing hours in, where you'll have the unique opportunity of being a human-sized fly on the wall in one cramped exam room after another, awkwardly standing in the corner with your hands in your pockets as you catch the patient casting uncomfortable glances at you.

You have to be a nuisance

In order to be a successful pre-med, you have to pester and cajole and plead to get what you need. Rare is the professor or doctor who responds quickly (or at all) to your first email; you may have to send several friendly reminders, followed by a visit or two to their office, to get them to respond. Pester too much, and they'll say no. Pester too little, and they'll forget you even contacted them. Pester them just right, and they still might say no. Regardless, you will become a doctor not just through hard work, but also from the good will and mercy of others.

Being a pre-med is costly

As a pre-med, you will be dropping some serious dough to pay for college and medical school materials. If you're on a full-ride scholarship, then congratulations! You don't have to worry about paying for tuition, meals, housing, or miscellaneous campus fees. That aside, every pre-med still has to pay a great deal of money to prepare for medical school. The MCAT, for instance, costs around $260 to register for a single test. Good test prep materials will run you about $2000. Your medical school application will charge you an average of $60 to apply to a medical school, followed by a $30-$100 secondary application per school. Volunteering abroad will require anywhere from $1500 to $5000 for just a couple of weeks, and studying abroad for a semester is rarely an option for a pre-med. For all of these things, financial assistance is lacking. You may knock a couple thousand dollars off your abroad trip, but very few qualify for financial assistance in paying for the tests and applications necessary to get into medical school. Ultimately, even with a full-ride, the average pre-med needs to pay around $3000 out of pocket just to be allowed to apply to medical school.

You are a slave to numbers

Your GPA, MCAT score, and résumé will rule your world as a pre-med, since they are practically the only things the admissions committees see when they look at your medical school application. You must carefully evaluate how you allocate your time between studying for class, studying for the MCAT, and extracurricular activities that demonstrate how much you love to serve the community. Students with excellent grades and MCAT scores may still not get into medical school simply because they did not demonstrate any kind of interest in helping others during their college years (e.g. volunteering with a fraternity, participating in mission trips, or working in the health services). Alternatively, students who live to serve others may not be in the running simply because their grades are sub-par.

The pre-med track is an unfair world, with very little time for personal life or solitude. You can expect to stay after class, shirk meetings, stay up late on weekends, and cancel dates to stay afloat on the tortuous river of long, hard work that awaits you. You will feel jealousy when you see your friends from high school take the easier roads to better pay. Being a doctor is a calling, and if you aren't called, you won't last. You must be a pre-med for yourself and no one else, or you will never survive the hardships that await you.

Reasons to Be a Pre-Med

"It has always been my belief that above potential, past experiences, or the obstacles we face, it is primarily our choices that determine who we become. I have found throughout my life that I could change many aspects of myself by making a decision and committing to it."

- An excerpt from my personal statement

Let us talk more about what you will be facing in the four years of college. In the previous chapter, I told you of all the woes that face pre-meds, but now let me share with you the best parts. After all, if being a pre-med were nothing but misery, no one would do it.

You are part of a team

Being a pre-med is analogous to being in a group of zombie apocalypse survivors, closely banded together against the trials that await them in the dark forest all around. Being a pre-med is tough, but you never have to walk the path alone. Next to you, ahead of you, and behind you are those who face the same trials as you, and that creates a strong sense of community. Out of the 21,000 total students at WKU, I would estimate that less than fifty power through into medical school, and I know them all very well. We study together, we go out together, we apply together, we encourage each other, and even when we have to separate and do things on our own, we have each other's backs. The pressures of the pre-med track forge the strongest friendships, some of which blossom into something more. I have seen some of the most beautiful relationships emerge from this life; your cohorts are your family, and someone very special may even join your family. Think about it: you spend so much time together, tend to have the same interests, and are on the same career track, maybe even to the same medical school and residency. If that isn't a great way to meet your match, I don't know what is.

You meet fascinating people

Not only do you become close with your colleagues, but you also become close with many professors. If you make the effort to go to their office hours and get to know them, professors can become great friends, mentors, and resources for your career. If you do research with a professor for an extended period of time, you are very likely to make a friend. I know pre-meds who babysit their professor's kids, brew beer with them on the weekends, go to church together, and generally become part of the family. I have a friend who shares an almost-unhealthy obsession about Transformers with a professor, and even though he is in medical school now, they still keep in touch. The Ph.D's whose lectures sometimes bore you in class are also some of the most interesting people you will ever meet. Go to their office hours, get to know them, and when it comes time to get letters of recommendation for a scholarship or application, they will be there to vouch for you.

All this applies just as equally to physicians who you shadow regularly. As you get to know the amazing people who have made medicine their life's work, they will offer you insights into the world of a doctor that you just can't get anywhere else. Some doctors are more willing to be a mentor than others, but the willing ones are worth taking the time to find.

You are forced to get involved

This may not sound like a benefit at first, but hear me out. It is easy in some fields of study to become detached from the community around you, but in order to be competitive for medical school, you *have* to get involved in community service. Not only that, you must also understand that being a pre-med requires that you demonstrate some ability to lead, and it tends to be the case that the most prestigious student leaders in the area (such as club presidents, club founders, or the bigwigs of student government) are pre-meds. It may be difficult to imagine how a pre-med could have time to assume those roles, but you will become a master of time management as you get more semesters under your belt. Being a leader in the community is an immensely rewarding thing to do, and you as a pre-med are most definitely suited to the task.

You are a community leader

The Medical College Admission Test (MCAT) has added a section to test you on the social and behavioral sciences just so you can demonstrate that you know what makes people and society tick. Doctors today are not just medical scientists, but are also expected to take the initiative in the community at large. As a pre-med, you will also be expected to lead your fellow students.

I was told recently of a physician from Ecuador who was sent on a medical mission trip to serve as the sole healthcare provider for a small Amazonian village for two years. Having just left medical school, this doctor was new and very nervous. When he finally made it through the dense woods and hills to the small village, the townspeople held a great festival for his arrival. Unbeknownst to him, it was the custom of this village to make the visiting physician also the mayor of the town. For two years, this newly-christened doc was also the mayor of a village.

Even if you are not the mayor of a town, you still have the power to implement incredible changes to a community. My uncle, Dr. Jack Scaff, a cardiologist in Honolulu, started and runs both the Honolulu Marathon and the Honolulu Marathon Clinic, an organization dedicated to getting people started on running marathons. Running with a community is a fun and effective way to get healthy, and my uncle recognized that. You too will have the potential to do something incredible with your doctorate in medicine; however, you do not need to be a physician to start making a difference.

I mentioned in the previous chapter that no one really cares if you're a pre-med, but I was referring specifically to college students and faculty. If you go on medical mission trips, you will likely command a great deal of respect from those you serve. One of the most popular (and most expensive) pre-med abroad trips offered at WKU is a trip to Kenya, where for two weeks you tend to the sick and injured at a small student-run clinic. When you arrive there, the townspeople greet you with a hero's entrance and bring you patients who have not seen the doctor since this trip was made the year before. Some will come in with injuries that require your direct intervention, some with simple illnesses, and some will be wheeled straight into your exam room in a blanketed wheelbarrow, and even if you just take the person's vitals or inject a drug, you will be the subject of much gratitude. I am told by my friends who went that it is a great way to strengthen one's resolve to pursue medicine. Remember that in many communities, particularly third-world communities, no one cares if you are a physician or not, because many don't even know what a physician is. They only care that you have a pair of willing hands that are there to make them feel better.

You get to do awesome stuff

Even if, like me, you cannot afford to study abroad, you still have the opportunity to watch and even participate in some fascinating medical procedures. Surgery shadowing is one of the most fun things for a pre-med to do, as it displays anatomy in a way you've never seen before, and shows what people can do to get the human machine working properly again. Last semester, I even had the opportunity to work a da Vinci robotic surgery machine, where I sat at a console and operated the billion-dollar surgical robot across the room. As a very hands-on person, I was in hog heaven using this device to perform some simple tasks like putting a rubber band on a cone. It may not sound that cool, but I would encourage you to try it yourself. It is an incredible experience.

Shadowing aside, your classes will regularly have you performing experiments in laboratories, ranging from modeling collisions to controlling chemical reactions to growing bacterial colonies to dissecting unusual animals. You will have plenty to do, particularly if you do research in a field of interest, and all of it will keep your hands and mind alive with new and fascinating information. Few people ever see the inside of a lab, but you will get clearance to operate electron microscopes, centrifuges, Nuclear Magnetic Resonance Spectroscopy machines, lasers, sonicators, autoclaves, and many more cool toys. You will learn what molecule types smell horrible and what smell great, and you'll get to see them all in action. Granted, every minute in a lab means ten more words on your lab report, but paper comes before work.

You have a chance at medicine

When the darkest times in my pre-med career bear down on me, this is the one thing that keeps me going. Sometimes I have to tell myself over and over that the purpose of my struggle is to have a chance at the career I have dreamed of since I was a child.

Medicine is a calling. This path is not something one of sound mind chooses for any other reason than to help others. There are several other reasons that I have outlined here as to why medical school is a good goal to pursue, but without being called to medicine one cannot expect to be satisfied by the other benefits. Long hours and hard work await you. Above all, to make it through to medical school, you have to want it.

Studying and Classwork

"It is 2:37 in the morning. The glow of a computer screen lights up your face as you make your apologies, full of the most sincere sorrow and remorse, for whatever it was you did in your past life that has so angered the great Mathematica gods. With only a cup of hours-cold coffee for company and lacking the energy to climb out of bed and get more, hope is fading quickly. Resigning yourself to the inevitable truth that 30 more minutes of staring at a block of errors will not, in fact, help you figure out what might be wrong, you retreat into the comforting arms of Facebook.

It is there that you find a message from your final project partner, sent at 2:13. 'Hey', it says, 'The bad news is, I still haven't figured out why the second screen won't pop up. The good news is I found this video of a baby sloth. Bonus feature: the sloth looks like it's wearing pajamas. Message me if you figure anything out.'"

This is an excerpt of the speech delivered by Curtlyn Kramer, a student in the class after me at the Gatton Academy, during their commencement ceremony. The quote is perhaps the best image of life as a pre-med that I've ever heard. Granted, some students choose to study in the mornings and go to bed early (like myself), but there still will be those nights when you have to stay up late and get things done. On those nights, it's easy to feel like you are the only one in the world who is struggling. But you're not. You never are.

One of the most important characteristics of a successful pre-med is his or her ability to shoulder a heavy load of coursework. Being successful in your classes requires dedication, efficiency, and practice.

If you are like me, you never really had to study much in high school. Your parents and friends were likely impressed by your ability to pick up information quickly and ace your exams while only rarely having to study. So far, you may have relied on your intellect to get you through the tough times of academia. Unfortunately, upon entering college, that time comes to an abrupt end. You may find that you are ill-prepared to handle the amount of studying you have to do to stay competitive for medical school. And remember, the main point of undergraduate college for pre-meds is to train you to absorb large amounts of information quickly, because there will be no time to learn that skill in medical school.

Pre-meds do not live a normal college life, as I mentioned elsewhere in this book. If you follow the normal academic track (i.e., entering college with little to no pre-college credit), then this is what you will likely be taking each semester.

Freshman Semester 1	Hours	Freshman Semester 2	Hours
Introductory Biology Course 1	3	Introductory Biology Course 2	3
General (Inorganic) Chemistry 1	3	General (Inorganic) Chemistry 2	3
Intro Bio 1 Lab	1	Intro Bio 2 Lab	1
Intro Chem 1 Lab	1	Intro Chem 2 Lab	1
Mathematics	3	Mathematics or Calculus	3
General Electives	4	General Electives	4
Total Hours	15	Total Hours	15

Sophomore Semester 1	Hours	Sophomore Semester 2	Hours
Cellular Biology	3	Zoology or Bio Elective	3
Organic Chemistry 1	3	Organic Chemistry 2	3
Physics 1	3	Physics 2	3
Cell Bio Lab	1	Zoo/Elective Lab	1
Orgo Chem 1 Lab	1	Orgo Chem 2 Lab	1
Physics 1 Lab	1	Physics 2 Lab	1
General Elective	3	General Elective	3
Total Hours	15	Total Hours	15

Junior Semester 1	Hours	Junior Semester 2	Hours
Animal Physiology or Bio Elective	3	Biology Elective	3
Biochemistry 1	3	Biochemistry 2	3
Molecular Biology or Bio Elective	3	Psychology or Sociology	3
Animal Phys/Elective Lab	1	Bio Elective Lab	1
Biochem 1 Lab	1	Biochem 2 Lab	1
Mol Bio/Elective Lab	1	Psych/Soc Lab	1
General Elective	3	General Elective	3
Total Hours	15	Total Hours	15

Senior Semester 1	Hours	Senior Semester 2	Hours
Anatomy	3	Histology	3
Immunology	3	Histology Lab	3
Parasitology	3	Graduation Requirements	6
Anatomy Lab	1	Senioritis	0
Immunology Lab	1		
Parasitology Lab	1		
General Elective	3		
Total Hours	15	Total Hours	12

As you can see, it's a lot of work. Each of these courses will be a unique challenge to conquer. Some will be easier than others, but you can be assured that you will have at least one course every semester that will cause you to question your decision to pursue medicine. You get better at handling the workload over time, but bear in mind that professors know that too, which is why they will pile on more and harder work in the upper-level classes.

But now, it is most prudent to break down the courses you will take into two categories: concept-based and application-based.

Concept-based courses

This is the primary type of course you will encounter in your biology and gen-ed curricula. In classes such as US History, Cellular Biology, Biochemistry, Art History, and Parasitology, you will swallow a lot of information and spit it out on the test. Often, the information you are being asked to remember will be difficult to associate with other things that were taught to you in the class. For instance, in biochemistry, the enzymes that perform certain vital processes in the body are named after the *opposite reaction* than the one they perform. This is because when the enzyme was first discovered, it was observed performing a reaction that became its namesake, even if the observed reaction was not the one it most often performs in the body. Yet, despite the fact that the name is wrong, you are still expected to know it. Confused yet?

If you took AP courses in high school, then odds are that you will know how to handle yourself in the introductory conceptual courses of college. The key to these courses is to improve your ability to memorize large quantities of information rapidly, and know what is important and what is not. Here are my tips for surviving the concept-based courses:

1. *Do the textbook readings.*

Often, students will skip the textbook readings if they are not absolutely required by the professor. Their reasoning is something like "My professor is just covering the same stuff in class, so why should I cover the same stuff again?" When I put it that way, you can already see the answer: Because that's what studying is. When you read the textbook – before or after the material is covered in class, your choice – you are forcing your mind to review the same information a second time, and that tends to make more stuff stick. Also, the book will explain the same things your professor talks about in a slightly different way, allowing you to learn the same material in two voices. Finally, the textbook has helpful pictures that can give you visual learners the perspective you need.

2. *Join or form a study group as early as possible.*

This cannot be stressed enough, and is perhaps the most important piece of advice I can give you as a pre-med. The students who survive this curriculum are not the lone wolves who feel like they can tackle all their classes by themselves, but rather the pack wolves, if you will, who take the time to bounce ideas off each other and instruct one another. If you are struggling on a particular concept in class, for example, and the professor just isn't explaining it in a way you understand, then ask people in your study group to help you figure it out. Once you understand it, then teach other people in your group.

Teaching others is a great way to learn the material yourself.

3. *Get to know your professor.*

Don't just pay attention to what the professor says in class; actually *listen* for verbal cues that will tell you what material the professor believes is most important to know (and, therefore, what he or she will ask you on the test). If the prof glosses over the mating habits of sea stars but really zeroes in on how the shell of a beetle is formed, then you should probably focus your efforts on the beetle shell. Don't forget, you can (and should!) go to the professor's office hours to cover material you're confused about. Doing so will also offer you the opportunity to get to know that professor, and to get him or her to like you. Professors aren't usually so emotional that they will give you a better grade simply because they like you, but they will certainly be more willing to go out of their way to help you if you are struggling on something. Rapport means support.

4. *Use mnemonics and songs whenever possible.*

Yes, this sounds a bit silly. Who would want to walk through campus singing the Krebs cycle song to themselves while people cast puzzled glances in their direction? (Been there, done that.) Songs and mnemonics really are like shortcuts in your brain to remember things. I still remember the quadratic equation because my teacher taught us a silly song about it six years ago! Use them whenever possible. If you have difficulty remembering something, look to see if there's a song for it online. The sillier it is, the more likely you will remember it.

5. *Take notes. Always.*

In the classroom, you have the opportunity to learn the same information twice. You first learn it when you see it on the professor's slide or hear them talk about it, and you learn it a second time when you write it down. In your introductory classes, you can expect most professors to upload a set of slides that you can print out before coming to class. However, using slides as your notes precludes the chance at taking notes yourself. Even if you have the slide show in front of you, grab a pen and write out the information in an organized way. Perhaps you don't end up using your notes to study for the exam, but you will still have better memorized the information if you took the time to write it out. When in doubt, write it down.

6. *Find your own way to study.*

Truthfully, the only sure way to get good at conceptual courses is to find your own way to learn. I have a friend who lounges on the couch and plays sitcoms in the background while he studies. Every time he hears a funny joke, his mind associates what he's reading with the joke, making it easier to remember. Personally, I need a desk, a straight-backed chair, and silence when studying, so I like to go to the library or just study in my room. I can also go to the crowded cafeteria to study; the white noise of many people talking at once is sometimes the best silence you can find. Some prefer to study most often in groups, while others prefer to study alone. Try several different types of studying and see what works for you.

7. *Learn how to take quick breaks when studying.*

When I was at the Gatton Academy, I was advised to take a fifteen-minute break for every forty-five minutes of studying. For the first two years of college, this proved to be a good rule for me and my classmates to live by; as such, I would advise you not to try to push yourself past a couple hours of straight studying. It is unlikely that you will retain much of what you studied in those marathon sessions. Later on in your college career, you will need to study more with less time, so the recommended fifteen minutes will not always be available. The best thing that works for me is a mini-break: When I feel my attention starting to wander, I pull out my smartphone and play a mindless game for a few minutes until I can tell that my attention has returned. In those mini-breaks, I would advise you against doing anything too cerebral, like reading an in-depth article, because your brain is already busy processing the information you're studying. Watch a funny video or have a lighthearted conversation before returning to the books.

8. *Learn to know when enough is enough.*

Your book is in front of you and your eyes are moving across the page, but nothing is sticking. You discover that you're reading the same sentence over and over again, but you just can't seem to get what the words are trying to say to you. You try a quick break, maybe even a long break, but when you come back, your mind is still fried. This is when you need to call it quits for the day. **You are not helping yourself by wasting your time pretending to study.** This is a crucial point with which some students have difficulty. If your brain is fried, then you are done. That's it. It doesn't matter if it's 2:00 PM the day before an exam; you will not be able to learn anything more until you allow yourself time for rest. Take a nap, or pull out a fun book to read, or play a video game. Watch a movie with a friend. Get your mind OFF of the books so it can begin to process what you have already learned.

Studying is analogous to exercise. Your body does not get stronger as you work out; rather, exercise exposes your body to harsh conditions that force it to allocate extra resources to improve your overall health. All the improvements come *after* you go to the gym, and they are directly affected by what you eat, what you drink, and how much you sleep. With studying, you will not be able to retain information if you are hungry, tired, or just not able to focus. Review and practice the material, and then shut your thinking cap off and go do something fun. While you are de-stressing, your subconscious mind is carefully organizing and storing what you have learned. Be careful, however, not to do anything too cerebral after you study, because you may find that you learned a heck of a lot about Armenian music or how to play a video game well instead of the cellular biology you were supposed to learn. Regardless, rest is *the most important* part of studying.

Application-based courses

This category primarily consists of math, physics, and analytical chemistry classes that are required for you to pass your MCAT (and graduate). There will not be too many of them that are absolutely required for you to take, but the ones you do need to take will teach you the analytical thinking process that is a must for every medical student.

Application-based classes do have a significant upside compared to concept-based classes: you do not have to blindly memorize the material covered in class. With a working knowledge of the field that you develop over time, you will ultimately be able to derive most any equation you need from one you already know. You will learn the ultimate tool of dimensional analysis that can help you understand mathematical relations between variables better than any memorization tool ever could. There are some people who have tried to apply their memorization skills from biology to these classes, and I have never known it to end well for them. Application-based courses require analytical and spatial thinking that is simply not developed in other courses.

Even so, my earlier advice for the conceptual-based courses still applies here, but let me also add a few points, straight from my experience as a physics tutor and teaching assistant:

9. *Learn the tool of dimensional analysis.*

Dimensional analysis is a strategy that will allow you to derive and create most any equation you need to make it through an exam in physics or chemistry, where units are paramount. It is the tactic of working through the units of an equation as if they are variables to see if you are using the right one.

For example, suppose I needed to determine how far a particle has traveled moving at a speed of 10 meters per second for twenty seconds. If you are a straight memorizer of equations, you may immediately pull up the equation that you learned in physics, "d=vt" (distance equals the product of velocity and time). However, suppose you didn't study that equation, but do remember the units of distance, velocity, and time? In this situation, dimensional analysis is your best bet. (Note: brackets denote units: *m* is meters, *s* is seconds.)

$$velocity \ v = \left[\frac{m}{s}\right]$$

And:

$$distance \ d = [m]$$

And:

$$time \ t = [s]$$

So in order to get an answer in meters (which is what the question asked for), I have to cancel out seconds, and I can do this by multiplying velocity and time.

$$v * t = \left[\frac{m}{s}\right] * [s] = [m] = d$$

Since the units of distance are in meters, it is *extremely* likely that the correct equation is d=vt. The units that so many pre-meds think are useless additions to make life harder on us are actually a helpful roadmap to the right equations and relations. If the units match, then it is likely that you have the right answer. *Remember this for the MCAT.*

10. *Ask yourself: Does my answer make sense?*

This may seem like something that doesn't need to be said: There are NOT one thousand kilometers in a meter. That just doesn't make sense. Yet, as a physics tutor and TA, I have had students give me answers just like that, and ones that are even more ridiculous, just because they didn't engage their common-sense circuits and ask themselves if what their calculator told them actually makes sense.

I often entertain myself by thinking what the world would be like if its ways were governed entirely by physics students who didn't bother to check their answers. It would go a little like this:

- If you toss a ball up in the air, it would immediately accelerate, crash through the roof, and punch a hole in the atmosphere faster than a bullet.

- If you stand on an inclined plane, you'd float right off into the sky like a beautiful bird.
- Cars would skid. Always.
- A horse would never be able to move a chariot. The chariot would just keep pulling back on the horse and stay rooted in place.
- If a leaf touched your hand, you would be slammed against the ground as if a truck had fallen on you.
- Transformers would magically create enough electricity to power the entire city of Chicago for two years.
- Pushing the accelerator on your car would cause you to fall into the ground at a colossal velocity.
- Pool would be the deadliest sport in existence.

Always be sure to ask if your answers make sense. It will save you a ton of points and extra work.

Note-taking strategies

The following is a short list of note-taking strategies I and my classmates use to quickly and efficiently note anything that the professor says or writes in lecture. For the sake of accuracy, I have removed more complex note-taking strategies such as Venn diagrams and webs; I have never met a single pre-professional who effectively used such strategies in upper level classes. All pre-professionals I have met take simple, highly adaptable approaches to note-taking. If it then helps you to re-copy your notes in a format of your choosing, then I would encourage you to do so. However, for classtime, you are likely going to want to use the strategies below.

Remember this cardinal rule for note-taking format: Put your notes on the floor, stand up, and look straight down at them. You will not be able to read the text, but you should still be able to see clear organization by topic, subtopic, and level of importance.

A. **Simple Concepts**

This is the bread-and-butter strategy for the pre-med. Simple, fast, easy to organize, and highly adaptable.

General format:

→ Primary Topic
- Information about this topic
- Subcategory about this topic
  → Subcategory information

Example:

→ Phospholipid Bilayer – membrane of cell
  – Composed of phospholipids
      → Phosphate head – hydrophilic, faces out of membrane
      → Fatty acid tails – hydrophobic, faces into membrane
  – Also contains proteins
      → Transmembrane – spans entire membrane
          • Used to move nutrients, provide stability
      → Structural – provides support
      → Signaling – used in immune response, cell communication

Possible modifications you may employ include circling important information, putting stars or names of topics in the margin to organize at a glance, putting dotted line breaks across the page when the professor goes off on a tangent or gives an example, and starting a new sheet of paper when the professor moves on to a new topic.

B. **Comparison or Organization of Concepts**

In those rare situations when the professor displays information in a logical, easy-to-follow manner, you should be able to use this tactic to quickly organize and compare information presented to you in class.

General format:

Categories	Criterion A	Criterion B	Criterion C
Category 1	Info	Info	Info
Category 2	Info	Info	Info

Example:

Phylum	Symmetry	Organization	Nerve System
Porifera	None	Cellular	None
Cnidaria	Radial	Tissue	Nerve net

Don't forget to leave additional space in the rows and columns in the event that your professor adds something that they feel is important during lecture.

C. Calculation-Based Notes

Example:

Surface Area Eq'n

$$A = \pi r^2$$

→ A = surface area of circle
→ $\pi = 3.14$
→ r = radius of circle

eg-

Circle w/radius r = 2 cm

Then,

$$A = (3.14)(2)^2 = 12.6\ cm^2$$

Simple and sweet, this way of writing equations and the examples that follow is an old standby for the pre-professional. If it is an important equation, make sure to put it in a box or circle, since professors will often derive more complex equations with a whole lot of fluff that you do not need to study for the test. As a result, the final equation can be difficult to find when you are studying if you do not make it stand out on the page.

Note how I abbreviated the word "Equation" with "Eq'n". It may seem like a small point, but this is actually a critical thing that can save you time when taking notes in class. You do not always need to write out the full word if an abbreviation conveys the same message. On the flipside, however, you do not want to write abbreviations that you know will confuse you later on (for instance, writing n to mean refractive index in one place, and then writing n to mean number of data points elsewhere). Remember, the goal here is to write smarter, not just faster.

Let me wrap up this chapter with one piece of advice that you will hear time and time again: Do your work on time. College is a time of your life in which you are thrown into a vast pool of information and told to keep your head above water. You are in an environment designed to test your ability to survive, and it's your responsibility to keep moving no matter what. If you manage your time responsibly, take breaks when you need them, and ask for help, you will be able to handle the immense workload of the pre-professional.

Building your Résumé

When you first arrive at college and meet all the incredible people who share your major, you may feel a sense of humility knowing you are no longer the head of the pack. As you get to know your classmates, you will begin to see the five types of pre-meds that will exist in your class: Show-Offs, Gunners, Textbooks, Givers, and Survivors.

The Show-Off

The Show-Off is the first pre-med to be eliminated. This is the proverbial student who walks into the first day of class with a palpable air of arrogance. Those who ask this person about their choice of major will receive an upturned nose and a clipped "I'm a pre-med" in response. Often, if you were to ask this student why he or she wanted to be a doctor, they would say something quite stock, i.e., saving lives and helping people. Truthfully, though, they may instead be after the glamour and cold, hard cash of being a leader in medicine. Once they truly have to struggle in class for the first time, or take a shadowing opportunity and see what a messy business medicine can be, this pre-med often changes their tune (and their major).

Before committing needlessly to a semester or two of hard classwork, try to persuade yourself *not* to become a doctor. Read my chapter on "Reasons Not to Be a Pre-Med", and listen to the horror stories from those you know who are involved in medicine. Ask yourself, truthfully, what attracts you about the job, and do some shadowing. Explore and determine if this is truly the path you wish to take, because if it isn't, it is better to find out sooner and save yourself some trouble.

The Gunner

The Gunner is the brownnosing pre-med who is totally focused on beating the competition for medical school. There are often a small handful of these, especially in the first year, who would gladly throw their classmates under the bus just to get a small lead. They do not work well with other students and only get involved with community service for the pads on their résumé. Due to the enemies they make, Gunners often do not stay in the major much past sophomore year.

The most important thing to understand about being a pre-med is that *it is not a competition.* Yes, all pre-meds are technically vying against each other for a limited number of medical school seats, but the scale of that competition is far larger than the handful of pre-medical students at your university. In working together with your colleagues, you will make yourself a stronger candidate for medical school. Being a Gunner means that you have to forage through the entire curriculum of pre-medicine on your own, and that is close to impossible. Be there for your classmates, and they will be there for you.

The Textbook

The Textbook pre-med believes that the only way to succeed in medicine is through raw knowledge. They are the ones who only have two modes (study and sleep) and they are totally devoted to their GPA and MCAT score. Often, you will feel like you are slipping behind in class because you see how much better they are doing. Textbooks may be attracted to medicine for the intellectual challenge alone. The cost of this approach, however, is a complete disregard for shadowing and extracurricular activities. Some of these students will make it into medical school, but most will be surprised when their application is rejected, despite the high numbers they have earned.

Being a good candidate for medical school is as much about community leadership as it is about book smarts. You must show schools that you are not only a capable student, but also a person who is devoted to the service of others. Prove this by getting involved in volunteer organizations you enjoy, and by earning leadership roles in those organizations.

The Giver

The Giver is the opposite of the Textbook; someone who enjoys community service, but has difficulty paying attention in the classroom. They may be known to skip class to sleep in after a night at the animal shelter, and their grades pay the price for it. Without sufficiently impressive grades, the Giver runs the risk of their application being waitlisted or rejected.

Medical schools have publicly said many times that the first thing they look at in an application is the GPA and MCAT score of the student. If those numbers are wholly unsatisfactory, the rest of the application doesn't even get a glance. These two precious numbers are your foot in the door, and it is essential that you take care of them. That is why the Giver, while having the heart of a doctor, needs to show that they have the academic dedication of a doctor too.

The Survivor

Finally, there is the Survivor, and this is the type of pre-med which will constitute the majority of those accepted into medical school. This is the one who has seen some of the not-so-fun parts of being a doctor, such as the veritable mountains of paperwork, and understands what a hard road this career is. They have asked themselves the hard questions and have chosen, no matter the difficulty, to pursue medical school. Survivors also establish a daily routine that allows them to keep swimming without feeling like they are drowning, and have become as comfortable as they can be with the hard work and long hours required. Balancing volunteer work with school, they also know when enough is enough, and where their limits are.

Survivors understand the value of asking for help. They are not afraid to admit when they are wrong, and when they need a fellow classmate to explain a concept to them. They have learned to swallow their pride and have accepted that while they may not always be the best, they will still push themselves. They also know that they may not get into medical school on the first try, but will continue to try for as long as it takes.

You will not know on the first day of school if you are a Survivor. That knowledge comes after you have survived a stressful semester or two that truly tested your limits. I have seen students literally banging their head on the desk in the middle of chemistry, shouting "I can't do this anymore!" And you can always find out how difficult an exam is by counting the number of students in the "defeat" posture: arms crossed on the desk, head in their arms. This is when you find out if medicine is right for you. If you take these hits and keep on running, straight through to the finish line, then you have chosen the right career.

I have asked medical students and doctors why medical schools view it to be so necessary to put pre-meds through difficult coursework for four years, and to still expect them to volunteer, do research, and shadow on top of that. The doctors I have shadowed told me that they have forgotten just about everything they learned in classes like organic chemistry, biophysics, and calculus, so why force students to take these courses if they are not directly relevant to the curriculum of life-saving?

The answer, from what I have been told, is that from the first day of medical school you are learning material that could potentially save a patient's life in the future, or keep them from unnecessary pain. You will feel like you are trying to drink from a fire hose; the sheer force of the information being propelled in your direction will leave you winded, even after your difficult experiences as a pre-med. In medical school, there is absolutely no time to learn how to study, how to manage your time, or whether or not this is the right career for you. As unglamorous as it seems, being a pre-med is all about training you how to be a medical student.

To be a Survivor of the pre-med meat grinder, you must synthesize the positive qualities of the Textbook, the Gunner, and the Giver, while totally avoiding those of the Show-Off. You must sell yourself to medical schools, and persuade them that you would make an excellent physician. My advice on how to do this constitutes the remainder of this chapter.

Take difficult classes together

Medical school applications committee members are particularly fond of enunciating this point. They want to see that you can handle multiple tough courses at the same time, because that will prove to them that you are capable of juggling your time, stress, and coursework, which is an essential criterion for a successful medical student. To that end, do not space out your hard courses over multiple semesters; take some of them together.

Get involved in research

One of the greatest opportunities you have as a student in college is getting involved in real-life research projects focused on fields that you enjoy. It is also a great boon to your medical school applications (particularly if you're going the M.D./Ph.D. route), so begin thinking about research early on.

Research is not nearly as intimidating as you might think it is without having done it before. It is also not as easy as movies make it appear to be. Instead of watching a short montage of people in white lab coats swirling fluid in Erlenmeyer flasks and tapping on a computer, you will be *in* that montage, and often the project you will be working on is so esoteric that most people outside of the lab have no idea what you are talking about. Forget dreaming up some green fluid to turn you into a superhero; you will instead be characterizing the genome of a bacteriophage by extraction and purification of DNA, cutting with enzymes, and examining the segments by mass in gel electrophoresis.

And it will be a hell of a lot of fun if you choose the right project.

If you didn't understand what I said above, do not worry. That is the type of stuff you will learn in the pre-med curriculum over four years of study. You also do not have to fully understand everything you are doing in the lab to be a good first-year lab technician. It's the difference between being an automotive mechanic and being an automotive engineer: the mechanic knows where parts go, and how to fix some of them, but the engineer knows how they all work together. In research, you are the mechanic and your professor is the engineer.

Choosing a good research project is like choosing a good doctor to shadow: it is all about what you are interested in, and who you can get along with. You may want to work with the eccentric genius who works with electron microscopes in the basement, or you might be interested in working with the calm, paternal biochemistry professor. If you like the professor, you will not need much more persuasion to like his or her research project.

Virtually every science professor at a university is involved with some form of research. They may talk about their work during lecture, and might even invite a few students who show promise to work with them. That is rare, however, and it is conventional for students who are interested in a professor's research to approach them. As you take your science courses, do not be afraid to ask questions about their research after class or during office hours. Professors are often so excited to talk about their projects with bright students that even showing interest gets you a foot in the door. It is always a good idea to get to know your professors, too, because you never know when you might need a letter of recommendation. Moreover, you will be spending a lot of one-on-one lab time with your research mentor, so it is important that you both get along.

Some universities offer research-oriented classes. If your university is one of them, I would highly encourage you to take one. In my first year of Gatton, I undertook a class-based genomics research project where I worked with bacteriophages (viruses that infect bacteria). I purified a unique phage from a soil sample I took from my backyard, named it, did some preliminary characterization of it, and added it to the Howard Hughes Medical Institute database. Most universities offer a similar, less intensive course where they just show you how to operate lab equipment and practice proper techniques. Once you have that information down, you can work with a professor even if you do not yet understand the advance science involved. Lab work is like cooking: you are given a recipe and specific steps to follow, and if you follow them, you often get an accurate result. Professors may initially have you running centrifuges, diluting samples, performing spectroscopy, or just cleaning glassware. Later in your college years, you will likely understand much more about the project and be able to go off in your own directions with relative autonomy, but no professor expects much from a first- or second-year lab rat. They often just appreciate your hard work and desire to learn.

Research internships, like studying abroad or summer programs, are big boons to your medical school application – particularly if they influenced you in some way. Be prepared to talk about any and all honors you receive as an undergraduate scientist, including internships, grants, and publications. Publications are an important step for any researcher; each is a medal of recognition from the scientific community. If you get your name in a research journal, count on mentioning that in your application.

Shadow, all the time

This activity is by far the best way to determine if medicine is right for you, and medical schools know that. They want you to experience the excitement and stress, but also the boredom, of being a physician in the modern world. They want to see that you know what you are talking about when you say you want to be a doctor. It is for all these reasons that every shadowing experience you have had, including an uneventful two-hour stint in the ER that you had a few years back, should be documented on your application.

Shadowing is also the hardest thing to get involved with if you do not have connections in the medical field. Those of you who work in healthcare will not have an issue with shadowing, as you already work with doctors firsthand, but those of you who do not will have trouble getting in touch with doctors. I received my EMT certification three years ago, but was unable to use it before it expired because no agency would hire me. I later learned that it wasn't because they didn't like how I cut my hair, but rather because other applicants had the connections; someone had a mom who worked at the hospital, or had a friend in the clinic, and these people vouched for them. I, on the other hand, was an unknown entity. In the same way, you may find yourself frustratingly stymied by medical bureaucracy when you try to get in touch with doctors to shadow.

Firstly, if you have connections, use them. Call up that long-lost uncle and ask to shadow him or his colleagues, *even if you have no interest in their field.* Who knows? You might love it, and any shadowing is good for the books. Ask anyone you know who works in the medical field if they can put you in touch with physicians. Heck, ask your *own* physicians that you visit if you can shadow them. If you do not have connections, start making some. Go on hospital or medical school tours with your local pre-med organization, ask your pre-med professors, or just call up the front desk of some nearby clinic and ask if you can shadow there. It is your responsibility to find doctors to shadow.

Most importantly, *be politely persistent*. This is the only way you will get shadowing hours. Doctors and medical personnel are extremely busy people, and if you sent one an email about shadowing a week ago with no reply, it has likely been pushed to the bottom of the stack. They will need friendly reminders, sometimes for months after the initial email, before they finally get around to working with you. Phone calls are golden, because if they pick up, then they have to deal with you then and there. You will have to sign a form for HIPAA (essentially a patient privacy agreement), and some places will want you to have certain vaccinations before you are allowed to shadow. One practice at which I shadowed required me to wear a lab coat and stethoscope. To this day I have no idea why because everyone, including the doctor I followed, was dressed in business casual.

In my experience, the absolute hardest place to get shadowing hours is the operating room. I know that most of us are interested in surgery, myself included, but unless you get very lucky, have previous connections, or know who to pester, you are very unlikely to get OR shadowing. I only got to shadow the OR when I was in a summer pre-med program at a medical school, and I was so excited that I stayed a full twelve-hour night shift. Surgeons are notoriously hard to contact, and operating rooms are places where untrained hands could kill. That liability alone makes any hospital extremely resistant to the idea of observers in such a sensitive area, much like if you wanted to get shadowing hours in the Neonatal Intensive Care Unit (NICU, pronounced "nik-yoo" – it's for brand new babies who are extremely sick).

When you do get shadowing hours, remember the two core rules of shadowing: First, during the time in which you shadow, **you are not a medical professional**. You are truly just a shadow of the doctor. Do exactly what they say, stand exactly where they say, wear exactly what they say, and if someone mistakes you for a nurse or doctor, *do not pretend that you are one*. I know that should go without saying, but believe it or not I have heard stories of pre-meds who had the idiocy to pretend they were a doctor or nurse, and ended up way over their head. If you pretend you are a doctor in the ER, for instance, you might find yourself ushered into a room where a patient is dying, and everyone is looking to you for instructions. Even if you did know what to do, perhaps from your EMT or nurse's assistant class, and performed the entire thing swimmingly, you could end up in jail instead of in medical school for false representation.

Second, **follow your privacy agreement**. Before shadowing anywhere, you are required to fill out a nondisclosure statement where you agree to essentially forget all names, faces, and personal details about the patients you see. You will have the privilege of seeing a great deal of their lives, from their social security number to the sensitive procedure they are undergoing. It is perfectly fine to talk shop about the procedure you saw, such as how the doctor excised the lesion or why this patient's body was responding so strangely to the medication, but you are not under any circumstances to disclose the names or any identifying information about the patients you see *to anyone*.

Period. This includes other healthcare personnel not directly affiliated with that patient's care. Doing so is a severe breach of patient privacy, and you could end up in prison.

Enjoy what you do

Selling yourself is often the most frustrating part of being a pre-med, since it requires that you take into account how an extracurricular activity will *look* in addition to how much you enjoy it. However, you should always enjoy the activities you choose.

The physician who authored the foreword of this book, Dr. Luke Murray, came to speak to a group of pre-meds at a summer program that I attended. Having attended the University of Kentucky, he spoke to us about some encounters that he had had with students from big-name medical schools like Johns Hopkins and Duke. He had imagined that most of them were class president of their university in addition to holding three other prestigious positions on-campus, but after speaking with many of them, he found one major commonality: they all picked something they enjoyed and stuck with it for all four years. One man had started in his freshman year as a volunteer EMT for a student-run ambulance service, and in his senior year he became one of the managers of that service. That was his only extracurricular activity, but it got him into Stanford University School of Medicine.

We all may not be fortunate enough to have such a unique volunteering opportunity available to us, but there are many other opportunities you will have to be a leader, such as student government, volunteer firefighting, fraternity leadership, church leadership, and club leadership. Universities also have a reputation for being quite open to the new ideas of students. Want to lead in a club that doesn't have a presence on that campus? Create the club. Email administrators of various departments, ask how you could make it happen, and go from there. You may find that your idea gains some serious steam from the student body.

In my senior year, with the desire to leave something behind after I graduate, I decided to start the WKU Swim Club. I had no idea how to start a club, though, so I went to the sports club administration office and asked them. Two months and several packets of paperwork later, the Swim Club was an official sports club, and it is still running strong under new leadership. After I had put in the work to create the club, it took on a life of its own; the members and officers took what I had made and built on to it. By the end of the first semester of its operation, I gave my presidency to another student, completely let go of the reins, and watched the club grow under its own power. It was a very rewarding feeling.

Regardless of whether or not you start your own organization, it is important to join the clubs that are already available to you, especially your local pre-med society. Getting involved with these clubs not only puts volunteer pads on your résumé, but also serves as an easy way to develop a circle of friends and associates. Organizations like these usually have lasted for many years and have a strong support system in the university, so if you are not interested in starting your own, it would be wise to pursue the rather competitive leadership roles in these clubs.

One very important thing to clarify: Leadership roles are important to medical schools because they show them how you take charge in difficult situations. Therefore, you could be president of your local pre-med chapter or even class president, but if you don't do anything with that authority, it will work against you on your application. Medical schools do not just want to know that you have a leadership role; they want you to *make a difference* in that role. Start a petition, organize community service events, work with student government to enact a new policy that benefits students, or just do well with business as usual.

Everything I have just said about standing out also applies to your choice of job. In the semester before I took the MCAT, I accepted a position as a physics tutor and teaching assistant, which was one of the best decisions I could have made. Not only is being a TA a position of leadership, but the entire job also cemented my knowledge of physics for the exam. I decided after the test to stay with the job because of how much I enjoyed getting people interested in the material that they were studying. In the same way, I hope you find the job that serves you and your application well.

Working in undergraduate positions on-campus, particularly in jobs that put you close to faculty, is a great way to network. It is almost as ideal as working in the healthcare profession itself; being an EMT, volunteer firefighter, or ER technician is a *huge* boon to anyone's medical school application. However, like in clubs, you should choose what you want to do and stick with it for a while. This demonstrates to medical schools that you have the ability and the willingness to commit to a profession.

Remember what's important

Know that while committing to a job or organization is a boon to your résumé, committing to your career is the most important thing. Those of you who are like me, and want to dip your toes into a lot of different worlds, will still be able to get into medical schools if you demonstrate to them that above all, you are committed to becoming a doctor. This means getting your classwork in on time, having a good GPA and MCAT score, and serving the community, even if that means you go through phases. I have been in over ten organizations for various periods of time while in college, yet most were focused on serving the community in different ways. I am sure that helped to mitigate the fact that I had difficulty sticking to just a few ventures.

Being a pre-med is partially about you wanting to be a doctor, and partially about you looking good for the camera. Your application is the only window that most medical schools will have into your life before they invite you for an interview, so make it shine. Make yourself an applicant who can't *not* be accepted. Take difficult classes together, get involved in research, shadow, enjoy what you do, and remember what's important. You are already a worthy applicant to medical schools. The only thing you have to do is demonstrate that through your actions.

Managing Stress

It has been said many times by the self-help community that the biggest enemy you have is yourself, and I am in complete agreement. The world of pre-medicine is filled with constant daily challenges; tests that force you to ask yourself if you are really cut out for this line of work. It is all designed to be that way: med schools want to know that you are one hundred percent committed to the medical track, and that you are capable of handling its challenges. They do not have the spare money or time to waste on someone who isn't cut out for the job, especially since they cannot refill your seat in that class after the first year of school begins. The motivation, therefore, for medical schools to pick the right people is at least understandable.

Unfortunately for us, that means that we pre-meds have to learn to manage a great deal of stress while our classmates have fun. Managing yourself is far and away the most difficult obstacle to overcome, and you must overcome it before going to medical school. College is the time to learn about yourself; medical school is the time to learn about medicine.

Manage your time

In order to manage your stress, you must first manage your time. As I mentioned at the end of the "Studying and Classwork" chapter, you must keep your head above water; if you let the work you have to do pile up, you will drown. The only way to survive in the pre-med world is to keep moving: to work in the present, plan for the future, and leave the past behind.

The first and best way to begin managing your time is to buy a planner, *now*, and learn to use it. Keep it open on your desk, or use a calendar. Regardless of how you do it, you must develop a pen-and-paper way to organize your time. Print out your class schedule and tape it to the wall in your room, so you can see what your daily obligations are at a glance. You will frequently have to plan meetings, appointments, and social events around your schedule, so having easy access to your times of availability is crucial.

In your freshman year, you should focus on finding the best way for you to study. The aforementioned "Studying and Classwork" chapter discusses studying in more detail, but here I will focus on *when* to study. Perhaps your mind performs best in the morning, or in the afternoon, or at 2:00 AM. Experiment with study times to see what works for you, but always allocate time in your day to study. The way that worked for me was to set study hours for myself: I wrote down specific times in my planner when I would do nothing but study. After I found what worked best for me, and trusted myself to set aside time to study, I stopped writing specific times. However, the best way to start learning to study is to use your planner.

The second way to manage your time is to purchase a small, inexpensive notebook and write down reminders for the day, such as reminders to work on a specific assignment, go to a meeting, or practice an instrument. Anything you might forget should be written down in this little book before the day begins. I don't go anywhere without it; I bring a pencil with me and write reminders for myself as I think of them. In the middle of class, I may remember that I need to buy something specific at the store, so I will begin a shopping list in the book. This is an extremely useful tool and I highly encourage you to use it.

For appearance's sake, you should always write your reminders on paper instead of in your phone. You will often find yourself needing to write down something when talking with people, and pulling out your phone looks very bad since people will automatically assume that you are texting. You want to make sure to project an image of attentiveness, even if what you are writing isn't germane to the discussion.

Finally, when a task is completed, literally cross it off on the paper. This may seem like a small point to make, but I cannot tell you how cathartic and stress-relieving it is to cross a task off of a list. I often will cover it up completely with scribbling so I don't have to look at it anymore. Be decisive: when the task is complete, cross it off and eject it from your brain. At the end of the day, you will see all the tasks you crossed off and realize just how productive you have been. The power of this little act on your psyche cannot be overstated, since the constant stream of incoming work will often make you feel as though you are spinning your wheels and getting nowhere.

Avoid unnecessary stressors

Yes, drama kings and queens, I'm looking at you. We all know how high school consists of four years of barely-contained soap opera, but you must begin to distance yourself from that from the moment you matriculate to college. The bored adolescent mind will find many ways to stay occupied, including righting perceived wrongs, going to bat for friends, and holding a big soggy bag of grudges. These unnecessary stressors will stand in the way of what you have to do.

Stress is not a feeling, in my opinion, but a resource. You have to budget stress like you budget your money, and the currency is the stressor: a small, unitless quantity of mental tension. You have a limited capacity for stress, and you will discover this limit pretty quickly. Unlike money, you want to minimize your amount of stress, and get rid of stress whenever possible. If you take on unnecessary obligations or mentally taxing activities, the stress you devote to those pursuits will force you to take mental resources from the most important obligations, such as class, shadowing, and leadership opportunities.

Avoid unnecessary stressors like you avoid unnecessary spending. If you are in a drama-filled relationship, get out. If you still have that friend who likes to turn everything into an argument, leave them behind. If you find yourself wasting your brainpower on unproductive thinking, ask yourself why, and try to change tracks to a line of thought that serves you better, such as reviewing what you covered today in class, considering what kind of doctor you might want to be, or thinking of something fun that can help relieve your stress. Drop the unnecessary baggage.

Learn when to say "no"

The quintessence of being a first-year in college is taking on too many obligations at once. At the end of last semester, I started a swim club here at WKU out of personal interest (and because it would look killer on my medical school applications). I had to scout for potential officers, but I eventually found people who wanted to serve as vice president, secretary, treasurer, and risk management officer. All were freshmen who were just finishing their first year in college.

This semester, they all still hold their titles, but not surprisingly, all but the current president (my successor) are inactive. Trying to get those officers to do much of anything is like pulling teeth, primarily because they are more busy than they thought they would be. I knew this was probably going to happen because, as I mentioned before, first-years are prone to putting too much on their plate.

If you are of an entrepreneurial spirit, then you will likely find yourself in the same situation. Maybe you started a new research opportunity that is demanding too much of your time. Maybe you have a new job that forces you to work long hours of overtime. The proper response in those situations is not to try to juggle more balls than you can, but rather to cut out the fat in your schedule. In other words, go up to the leaders of these organizations and respectfully resign your role. Explain to them the honest truth: that you thought you would have time for the responsibility, but have come to realize that you do not. Most will be understanding of the massive workload you bear, since pre-meds have something of a reputation for being busy bees.

There is another, more self-serving, reason to know when to say no. In most of your applications, whether they be for scholarships, internships, jobs, or medical schools, you will be asked to list your extracurricular activities, including when you started in an organization, when you left, and *why* you left. Saying you didn't have the time for the extra obligation is much better than saying the president kicked you out of your role for being inactive.

Exercise, and eat healthy

This is the single most effective way to relieve stress that I know of. I'm the kind of guy who has to struggle to get my butt down to the gym, but I do it three times a week because it effectively increases the amount of stress that I can handle. In the afternoons, I either go swimming or get on the treadmill. I do not particularly enjoy exercise, but without it, I would not be able to handle the obligations of my daily life.

Humans are animals, and have animal biochemistry. We are not designed to be physically inactive; sedentary lifestyles take a toll on our mental health whether we notice it or not. Even if you are one of the fortunate few who do not have to worry about weight gain, rigorous physical exercise serves a purpose to you that is far more important than just looking good. Regular exercise opens reward pathways in your brain that make life in general easier to handle. Exercising after an exam, for instance, puts you into an almost blissful state of internal peace, enabling you to get your mind off the questions you may or may not have missed. Throughout the day, these reward pathways are still open and keep your stress in check. Also, regular exercise activates your metabolism, and throughout the day, you will feel more energetic, more awake, and hungrier (which means you can eat more food!). If you are so inclined, regular exercise also gives you a very healthy libido.

If exercising is a problem for you, focus on making the most of your time at the gym. Set aside three times a week to go down to the gym, and focus on just going there for starters. Once you are there, you will find it relatively easy to exercise, but *getting to the gym* is the hardest part. Find a cardio workout that you enjoy (or can at least tolerate), such as ellipticals, swimming, biking, running, or crossfit.

I am a swimmer primarily, but sometimes I just do not feel like getting into the freezing cold water of the campus pool. Instead, I'll go down to the gym, get a bike machine, put on some of my favorite trance music and go for thirty minutes. Swimming is one of the most effective workouts at managing your stress and keeping you fit. I swim because it is the workout that gives you the most bang for your buck: the most exercise for the least time. Thirty minutes of hard work in the pool can equate to almost an hour on the running track in terms of calories burned and stress relief. If you want to swim, but do not know how, your college likely offers a short bi-term class that can teach you the essentials. Once you know how to do it, you'll never forget.

Eating healthy is the second essential part of staying sane. Fatty foods and unhealthy eating habits mess with your mind, especially if the food doesn't taste absolutely amazing. Fried and processed foods are tasty, but will end up making you feel off if you eat too much of them. With a healthy diet, you will find that you have more energy and overall satisfaction in your life.

Food is a major stress reliever when you pick the right stuff to eat, but that doesn't mean you have to choke down a plain salad or swallow oatmeal every morning. That is actually a harmful habit if it stresses you out. Your food should be an enjoyable part of your life, and if you know how to prepare food properly – even in the cafeteria – you will be able to have your health and like it too.

It is likely that your college has a pretty crappy selection of on-campus food to eat. If you are looking to eat healthy, you may just have to make your own food, since often campuses will provide pizza, burgers, soda, and packaged gas station food. The on-campus cafeteria will offer you nasty salads that are just not fun to eat, and that's about the only option you will have if you are looking to stay healthy.

Here are some great ways to eat healthy on a budget, while still being able to enjoy your food:

- Load up a salad with fresh lettuce, mixed chopped vegetables, clean protein like kidney beans or tofu, nuts or fried noodles for a crunchy feel, oil and vinegar for extra flavor, your favorite dressing, chopped fruit, and chunks of meat like ham or bacon. Experiment and find a salad you like. **If it doesn't taste good, you're not doing it right.**
- Grab some bags of frozen boneless, skinless chicken breasts from the local supermarket. That is about the cheapest and healthiest meat you can buy. Find a Hispanic grocery store in town; they sell spices for the lowest prices I have ever found. Wash the chicken breasts with cold water, rub some vegetable oil, chili powder, cumin, and garlic powder all over them and shove a big batch on a sheet into your dormitory's oven at 375 °F for an hour. Take them out, stick a meat thermometer into the thickest one and see if its internal temperature is 165 °F or above. If so, put the breasts into plastic containers and stick them in your fridge when they have cooled. Boil some pasta if you want, and get some marinara sauce

from the store. Microwave up some frozen veggies and you're in business! Congratulations: in less than two hours and for less than $20, you have just made dinner for the next week.

- Keep unhealthy snacks out of your room, because if they are there, you will eat them. Replace them with healthier snacks you enjoy, such as fruit strips, nuts, dark chocolate, veggies, fruit, and sugar-free chewing gum. (It isn't food, but it keeps my mouth occupied so I am not as tempted to eat.)

- Drink titanic quantities of water. Buy yourself a water-filtering pitcher and keep it filled and close by. Drinking water helps shut down midnight hunger pangs, keeps away headaches, and strengthens your immune system. Make some tea if you wish: In a dorm, this means that you need to get an electric water boiler (use your filtered water to prevent calcification in the boiler). Remember that plain black coffee also counts as water, so if you want caffeine, get a coffee maker without a glass carafe. Glass coffee carafes tend to break in the cramped confines of a dorm room.

Socialize

Always remember that you are in a small group of people struggling to make it through a difficult situation, and you cannot succeed without the help of others. The ones who make it through the hard courses of college are the ones who form study groups, quiz each other, air their frustrations together, compare answers to problems, and push each other to work harder. It may be possible for you to survive the first few classes of the pre-med curriculum without any help or support from others, but that will not last long. So, as soon as you begin a course you know may be difficult, get a study group together. Exchange phone numbers or other contact information, and keep each other in the loop.

Don't forget to go out with friends on the weekends and whenever you have time. Socializing is a great way to get your mind off schoolwork, which is one of the most difficult things to do when you are in the thick of a tough semester. Do not, however, get in the habit of going out with certain people just because you feel obligated to. That is one of the unnecessary stressors that you cannot afford in a tough major. Socialization should serve the purpose of lowering your stress levels, not raising them. Remember, your peace of mind comes first.

Lean on your faith

It gives a pre-med college student great strength to be able to lean on religious or spiritual belief. While I do not have a specific belief system at this time, I have seen the effects that strong faith has had on my colleagues and classmates; they are invariably more able to handle the stresses of college life. Whether they identify with a formal religion or not, the sense of community and internal peace that comes with spiritual belief can serve as a strong support system for your own sanity. Those who pray have the ability to talk to the one(s) they worship about what's going on in their life, which is therapeutic regardless of the divine response.

I have had pre-med friends who identify as Muslim, Wiccan, Christian, Atheist, Agnostic, Neopagan, and many other identifications, some of their own creation. Regardless of the belief system, identifying with a specific faith puts you in a tight-knit community of others who share that faith. This is an effective way to get a social circle together quickly, particularly if you are entering a college where you do not know anyone.

Case Studies

Time for some practice. Below are some case studies of situations you may encounter in your life as a pre-med. Review the situation and decide on the *least stressful* course of action. It may not be what you actually end up doing, but knowing what would minimize your stress is the first step towards doing it. While there are no "right" answers to these examples, they will nonetheless help prepare you to face similar situations in college.

a) A friend from high school constantly texts you in class and throughout the day, wondering what you're up to. They often vent to you about their problems and want you to reassure them. You have never had the heart to tell them how much that annoys you because you know they do not have a lot of friends, so you occasionally respond. However, the stress of this semester is bearing down on you and you are afraid you may snap at them.

b) Some time ago, you joined a small club on campus out of personal interest. The club meets during your regular study time, but the meetings are moderately fun to attend. You are considering taking an officer's position in the club next semester, which would require that you attend all meetings. This would give you a small pad to your résumé, but would also require some extra work. You are also not sure that you will have the time to spare next semester.

c) You are in a relationship with your high school sweetheart, but things have been rocky lately. You chose to go to college, and they chose to stay in their hometown, which is quite a long drive from where you attend college. You both are attempting to work the long-distance angle of the relationship, but you are now not so sure that you want to stay with them for the long haul. You feel yourself changing in your first year of college; you are getting older, but it seems that they are staying the same. (*Note*: This is a very common thing for first-years to experience.)

d) You are currently employed, and the job is beginning to wear on you. The hours are long, the pay is unimpressive, and your boss knows how to push your buttons. While you do not need the money that you earn from this job per se, the extra cash enables you to go out with friends and buy yourself gifts that lower your stress levels.

Relationships

Being a pre-med can be compared to being an astronaut on the International Space Station: you must ration every minute of your time, you are often doing things people on the outside only vaguely understand, and you live in zero gravity in a small station orbiting Earth.

Alright, that last part is not relevant to being a pre-med, but the rest is. Since you are on such a tight schedule, you must make sure that all your free time is being used to de-stress and catch up on the things that matter to you. This may include personal projects, friends, shows, books, and video games. However, if you are in a relationship, most of your limited free time will be spent with that person. It is definitely within your best interests to make sure that spending time with that person is enjoyable rather than a chore.

People have many reasons for entering into a relationship during their time in college. The most ideal reason is the one that is most often misunderstood: love. We would all like to believe that people enter into relationships for the express desire to be with the other person, and out of a willingness to commit to an extended period of time together, but that is not always the case. The conundrum of love and commitment could fill this entire book, but I have limited the scope of this chapter to how relationships can impact your pre-medical career.

In my freshman year of college, I was in a relationship with a great girl. We had a lot in common, and the conversation never grew dull. We spent a lot of time together; in fact, we spent too much time together. Being a solitary person by nature, I soon found myself annoyed at her wanting to be with me seemingly every minute that I was free. We talked about this issue, but never really seemed to get anywhere with it.

Conversely, she had a problem with my martyr mentality: being a hormonal and insecure teen, I would purposefully keep myself from doing things that made me happy because I thought I did not deserve to be happy. Taking pity on someone like that from afar is easy to do, but being in a relationship with them is much more complicated. With these problems, the relationship ultimately grew too argumentative for either of us to handle. Before I transferred back to WKU, we ended the relationship on good terms.

From that time we had together, and my time in other relationships, I learned a great deal about what it means to be part of a whole. I have come to realize that a good relationship boils down to five critical criteria: communication, compromise, commonality, personal strength, and timing.

Communication

Communication is the first indicator of a healthy relationship: both parties maintain a policy of complete honesty and openness with each other. A strong couple does not play games; if one person has an issue, they bring it up at an appropriate time and with the desire to talk it through rather than argue. In return, the partner listens actively, represses comebacks, and makes every effort to talk the issue through rather than start a fight. This will not always happen in every situation, but more often than not, you and your partner should be able to discuss relationship issues without turning it into an argument.

The best way to communicate with your partner is to listen actively. This is when your mind is focused on what the other person is saying, *not on gathering ammunition to throw at them.* Discussions with your significant other are not political debates, and you should not treat them as such. Besides, in a healthy relationship, neither you nor your significant other should hold on to things that happened in the past. Have you known people in relationships where one person will "forgive and forget" something that the other person did, but later on, he or she will bring it up in an argument?

In arguing, neither person is actually listening; rather, they are just looking to shout hurtful things at each other. Arguments do not facilitate communication, but instead just put more stress on the relationship. If you find that you and your significant other are arguing a lot, then try to ask yourself why. Have you both been under a lot of stress lately? Is some outside influence in your lives causing you to be at each other's throats? Or is it an unaddressed issue in the relationship itself?

If you find yourself in the middle of an argument with your significant other, remember that it takes two people to fight. Swallow your anger and instead focus on listening to what he or she is saying. Let them get it all out (without goading them) and then speak calmly. Start with a *sincere* apology ("I'm sorry I hurt you when I did that. That was stupid of me."), and follow up with a *sincere* positive remark ("I'm glad you brought this up so we can talk it through."). If the mood is still tense, then cease discussion and give yourselves both time to cool off. *You cannot effectively discuss relationship issues while angry.*

Compromise

After communication comes compromise, which is just as necessary to a healthy relationship. In order to be in a relationship with someone who is not quite literally your clone, you *must* be willing to compromise with them. This means *doing things you do not necessarily enjoy*. Part of being in a good relationship with anyone is being equally devoted to their happiness as you are to your own. Maybe you should go to their family reunion like they want you to, or avoid teasing them about something that upsets them. In return, they should also do nice things for you because they care about you. Compromise is agreeing to do something differently in return for them doing something differently, thereby allowing your relationship to proceed with less friction in the gears. It requires that you both swallow your pride, manage your temper, and learn to be a couple instead of two individuals.

Commonality

The next criterion to an effective relationship is not one over which you have direct control: commonality. This is perhaps the most obvious indicator to whether or not you and this other person would get along together, and it is easy to see. If you both find yourselves constantly enthralled in conversations with each other, and don't notice when hours go by, then that is a pretty good indicator of commonality. If you find yourself scrambling for things to talk about, or you both end up bored in each other's company, then you might re-think your intentions.

One of the best ways to determine commonality is the "comfortable silence". This is a much-envied state of comfort with another person where you can both sit there and not say a word for long stretches of time without any discomfort. When you are not comfortable with silence, you may find yourself babbling just to fill it. However, I have been in relationships so comfortable that we could literally stare into each other's eyes for thirty minutes without realizing we were doing it. It is important to understand that this milestone, while being a very good sign, is *not* a definitive indicator of love. Nor is it something that will be achieved overnight.

Another form of commonality that is equally as important is sexual compatibility. If you and your partner do not engage in any form of sexual activity, then you may safely skip this section, but the majority of college relationships will include some form of sex. Healthy sex is one of the best things you can do for yourself and your significant other. It combines exercise, de-stressing, and time with your significant other all into one incredibly fun and intimate experience. Of course, remember to always be safe by using a condom or other form of birth control.

There are many caveats to having sex, because it is obviously a very intimate thing to do with another person. First, for the majority of people, there is *no such thing* as casual sex. If you want to try being friends-with-benefits with someone else, know that ultimately one of you will likely develop feelings for the other person. When that comes to pass, that person will begin to disdain having to casually toss aside their intimate experiences with the other. This will inevitably lead to friction in the friendship, forcing it either to progress to a relationship or disappear entirely.

Personal strength

Personal strength is an enigmatic necessity to a relationship: you have to be independent to ultimately be dependent. One of the reasons that many of my relationships, including the one I mentioned before, failed in the past is because one or both of us *needed* to be in a relationship. I realized after I left for WKU that the girl I was with didn't necessarily <u>want</u> <u>me</u> for a partner, but rather <u>needed</u> <u>someone</u>. That someone, at that time, just happened to be me.

My motivations were not much different than hers. I was spending a year in a university seven hundred miles away from anyone I had ever known, and as such I was in desperate need of a social life. Entering into a relationship seemed like the perfect way to establish a social circle, but even after I realized I did not want to be with her, I could not muster the strength to break up. I was too stressed, too alone, and too insecure to handle the solitary life of an out-of-state student. That was precisely the reason I should have ended it sooner than I did.

Being in a relationship based on need will ultimately end in misery, if not failure. Using another person as an emotional crutch is easy to do as long as you are basically compatible; however, it will rarely progress to a healthy relationship. People do not want to be used; they want to love and be loved. In order to find the right one for you, you must first be able to stand on your own two feet. This means staying single for a period of time *after graduation from high school* to learn more about who you are and become comfortable in your own skin. It is most definitely an uncomfortable transformation, but when you have attained that level of self-awareness you will be able to refuse offers for relationships that you know would not go anywhere. You will also understand that you deserve to be happy in a relationship, and that you should not be with someone because you think they need you. With this comes the patience necessary to keep the door open for the right person to walk into your life. Time spent in a bad relationship is better spent with yourself.

Timing

Finally, the most critical factor to a successful relationship is the one that is completely out of your control: timing. Two people could have everything right for a relationship, but if the timing in their lives is off, it will fail. In order to get a good relationship going in most circumstances, you both must cross paths and *stay that way* for years or longer. You must be in the same place, at the same time, and at the right time in both of your lives to enter into a relationship. You must not be in other relationships (which is why I advise against being in ones that you know are not right for you). You also must have significant time, especially early on in the relationship, to spend together. The healthy relationship we all want requires timing that is nothing short of perfect.

Bad news, pre-meds: your timing is almost always bad. You are entering into a field of study where every day is a struggle, and time management is key. With your rigorous class load, and your extracurricular activities, it is virtually impossible for most pre-meds to give a relationship the time it deserves. Many pre-meds also end up going to different universities for medical school than the one they attended for their undergraduate degree, which further complicates the idea of a long-term healthy relationship.

Unless you are a very special type of person, do not even think of trying to pull off a long-distance relationship. As humans, we have a strong desire for the ones we care about to be in close proximity to us, especially our significant other. Given that we are also highly sexual beings, particularly in the teens and twenties, it does not help to be in a committed relationship with someone who is too far away to satisfy those needs. This situation puts a great deal of stress on most long-term relationships, and it often leads to one or both parties being unfaithful. Out of the hundreds of relationships I have seen during my time in college, I knew of only two that survived long-term long-distance. One of those ended in marriage, and both had years of history behind them before the long distance came into play. Save yourself some heartache and stick to relationships with people who will be around you for a while.

It may surprise you to learn that I have actually seen the majority of successful relationships form in medical school instead of college. I suppose this makes sense for a few reasons: first, you are in a small class of people who do not plan on going anywhere anytime soon (many will stay in the same city for years after they graduate). Second, you spend a great deal of time with the same people as you study and socialize together. Third, most medical students know what they want, and have sufficient self-confidence and stability to pursue a healthy relationship.

Love

You may have wondered why I did not add love to the necessary criteria for a healthy relationship. Movies and television seem to view love as an emotional attraction to someone else that is deeper that mere infatuation or lust. However I feel that attraction, while necessary, is not sufficient for love. Love in the mature sense is less of a feeling and more of a *choice*. It is a decision made by both parties in a relationship to stay with each other, no matter how hard the relationship may become. Love is a promise that when the shit hits the fan, you can count on the other person to be there for you, and you will be there for them.

To find out if you truly love someone, you must first be in a healthy relationship with them, even if that is a friendship. Then ask yourself if my good friend Logan Eckler's definition of love applies to you: "Anything good that happens to me, I wish would happen to them. Anything bad that happens to them, I wish would happen to me."

However, you cannot be sure that you love someone without weathering some rough spots together. The difference between the couples that make it and the couples that don't is not the circumstances that they have to deal with; it is *how they react* to those circumstances. Successful couples do not let the hard times turn them against each other, nor do they allow small things to fester and cause rifts in the relationship. Along with the five criteria I have described, they have a mutual decision to stay together even if they drive each other crazy at times. That decision, in my opinion, is love.

The reality of relationships

I do not have any illusions of the nature of college relationships; I know that for most of you reading this book, your experiences will differ dramatically from mine and those of my friends. I also know that it is far easier to read my advice in this book than to follow it when you are in the throes of college romance. Do not blame yourself if you make mistakes. Just do your best to only make the mistakes that you can come back from.

Take this chapter as a primer to your understanding of college relationships. Throughout your time in the undergraduate world, you will have opportunities for relationships, opportunities for sex, and maybe (if you're lucky) a shot at the real thing. Most pre-meds will stay single for the majority of their college career; if that should happen to you, do not think it is because you are unwanted or unattractive. Being a pre-med does not allow much time for meeting new people.

Regardless of whether or not you are in a relationship, you will always have a circle of friends and family to fall back on when times are tough. Like in every other aspect of pre-med life, do not feel that you are the only person going through rough spots. Because you aren't.

Paying for College

My financial history with college is a mosaic of need-based financial aid, work study, patchwork scholarships, and payments made by my parents. Though I did not contribute a meaningful amount of personal savings to tuition (seeing as I had no personal savings), many of my fellow pre-meds worked their way through college. Some worked for years prior to attending college just so they would have enough savings to make it all the way through.

I interviewed some of those students prior to writing this book. Most worked as waiters or tutors or medical technicians, and all the jobs they worked were part-time. Many spent their weekends and breaks amassing some extra cash for living expenses. Most did not live on campus after their sophomore year, nor did they take on any but the cheapest meal plans. All believed that they had learned a lot about managing their money throughout college and were more prepared for medical school as a result. However, these students all had some form of scholarship or loan in addition to what they earned.

To lay a successful financial foundation for college, I recommend you follow the tips I outline in this chapter. I am by no means an expert on money management, so you should also consult your university's financial aid and scholarship departments. The tips below are arranged in order of priority; you should worry about the first one first, and the last one last. The sooner you get all of them done, the sooner you can focus completely on your education.

Take stock of your resources

So you have just been accepted to your dream school and plan on going pre-med. Congratulations! Take this time to determine what money you have available to you. For instance,

1. Scholarships – How much money have you been awarded? Can you apply for any more scholarships?

    a. Keep in mind that every scholarship you are awarded when accepted to college is a one-time offer. If you are offered a full ride to a school but choose to go somewhere else, you will not be offered the same package again should you wish to transfer. You will have to re-apply to the school as a transfer student, and if you do receive a scholarship, it will likely be much less than what you were originally offered.

2. Need-Based Aid – At the beginning of every year, your family will be required to fill out a Free Application for Federal Student Aid (FAFSA). You personally will have to fill it out if you apply for aid as an independent. After applying, your university will award you a certain amount of need-based financial aid, usually in the form of loans or work-study (where you work for the university in exchange for tuition discounts). This is based partly on your family's Estimated Family Contribution, which is essentially how much money the federal government expects your family to front. (Whether or not your

family actually *can* give this amount of money is another story.)

3. Family Contribution – Going off of the previous point, how much would your family be willing to spend to keep you in college? Can you use family connections to get an inexpensive place to live (like living at home)? Perhaps you may work out a deal to buy a car from a relative? Do not be afraid to ask for their help; as a college student, you are not expected to be able to fully support yourself right out of the gate.

4. Personal Savings – Do you have any bonds or savings accounts you can use to pay for college? Remember, if you are being given aid by the government, they will expect you to dig in to whatever funds you have stored, even if you want to use that money for something else.

Consult the experts

Every university has a financial aid office dedicated to making sure you have the money you need to make it through college. This does not always mean that they will bend over backwards for you, but it does mean that you should take advantage of their experience and knowledge of the university's inner workings. When in doubt, defer to their advice.

As soon as you matriculate to college, you should get to know your financial aid department. Set up appointments with them as often as you set up appointments with your academic advisor. This will ensure that you know where and how you are getting your money.

Apply for jobs

Look up job listings on-campus at your university, and also off-campus if you have transportation. Be realistic with your choice of job: some jobs are too time-consuming for a pre-med, and you may not want to waste your time applying for overly competitive fields such as emergency medical services or phlebotomy. Common jobs that we all end up taking include waiter, cashier, tutor, Resident Assistant (RA), emergency room technician, hospital orderly, office worker, Teaching Assistant (TA), dormitory desk worker, and paid research assistant. Choose a job that works with your schedule and that you do not absolutely despise. Even if you do not need the money, having a part-time job shows medical schools that you can effectively manage your time between work and school. They have even been known to overlook the lower grade point averages of students who have to work many hours per week!

Tyler L. Scaff

Become a resident

One of the greatest ways to reduce bills as an out-of-state student at a public university is to attain residency in that state. That way, you are paying easily half of the tuition rates you pay out-of-state. However, this is extremely difficult to do. Residency requires a permanent living address (dorms do not count), a state-registered driver's license, proof of occupation, proof of intent to stay in that state for the foreseeable future, and a big chunk of cash up front. Many other out-of-state students will be working towards the same thing, so this may not be possible in some situations. I personally was not able to get residency in North Carolina while attending college there for all the reasons mentioned above.

116

Consider military service

Enrolling in your college's Reserve Officer Training Corps (ROTC) or enlisting in any branch of the military may take some time away from studying, but the scholarships they can give may be worth it. Just be sure you want to serve in the military; this goes for college scholarships as well as the Health Professions Scholarship Program (HPSP) that you can get while in medical school. Consult online pre-med forums and listen to the advice of those who have been through the programs.

Stay informed

This is an important piece of advice I give you from personal experience. When I initially matriculated to college at North Carolina, I did so with the understanding that the government would foot most of the bill through subsidized loans and university grants. (A quick note: Subsidized loans are loans that do not accrue interest until you graduate, as opposed to unsubsidized loans, which accrue interest from day one.) The expected family contribution from my parents was rather high, but we all figured we could manage for the next four years. However, when my first year there ended, I received notice that my expected family contribution had more than doubled for my sophomore year! Stunned, I asked the financial aid office why this had happened.

What I failed to realize was that the federal government took the following changes in our finances into account: first, my sister was set to graduate college in the fall. This did not impact us financially in the slightest since she was on a full-ride scholarship to an in-state university; however the federal government believed that this would allow us to pay for more of my tuition. Second, we had sold some stocks at the end of year 2011 to pay for my mother's shoulder surgery in early 2012 (and financial aid calculations do not take medical expenses into account at all). Those stocks were taken as income for that year, which means the EFC assumed we had that money to give to the government.

Finally, the federal government, in giving aid, also seems to assume that your parents are at or before that peak earning potential (that is, they have more free cash to spare than if they were older). This was not the case for my parents, who were in their sixties. Despite my pleading, there was very little else that the financial office of UNC-Chapel

Hill was willing to do. I transferred back to Western Kentucky University that year.

Do not allow your finances to rule you while in college. Like in class, always stay one step ahead of the workload, since that is by far the least stressful place to be. Try to get your finances in order before junior year so you can focus entirely on studying for the pre-med's biggest challenge: The Medical College Admission Test.

The MCAT

It was 7:30 AM on Thursday, May 22nd, 2014, and the sun was just cresting the Watterson overpass in the city of Louisville, Kentucky. My '09 Scion sang to me in electronic riffs and dubstep drops as I arrived at the four-story-high corporate cube, a building of black glass that would serve as my proving ground. I had driven this route the day before, right up to knocking on the door to make sure I had the right place, but that did not lessen the trepidation I felt as I approached the Prometric Testing Center on that cool morning. Thoughts and worry raced through my head.

What if I'm not ready? What if I have a panic attack? What if the questions are over topics I forgot to study? Oh my God, I don't want to have to do this again.

Stop it, Tyler. Easy, now. Just open the door, take your test, and leave. You'll be fine. You did just fine on the practice tests, and you'll do fine now.

But this is different! This is the real thing!

I wrestled my mind into submission as I made the short journey to the waiting room. *Down the hall, to the left, first door on your left.* A strange sense of relief washed over me as I entered a small, cramped waiting room already packed full of students trying to hide their terror.

"Is this where the party's at?" Nervous laughter followed my quip.

After checking in and storing my valuables in the locker provided to me, along with my customary 5-hour energy shot (half the first break, half the second) and two granola bars, I sat and made light conversation with my comrades-in-arms. I've always been good at keeping up appearances, and I think the other students appreciated my small talk. One by one, we were called into the next room for pre-test security procedures.

"Tyler Scaff?" My heart rate shot up from too-fast to Flash Gordon.

"Come on in, Tyler. Sit here, and let's get your fingerprints. Do you have everything out of your pockets? Good. Whoops, the fingerprint scanner isn't working too well today. Let's try that again. Alright, now stand up and turn out your pockets. Stand over here; let me wand you to make sure you're not carrying anything you shouldn't be. Turn around and put your arms up. Thank you! You are cleared to enter."

The test administrator led me into a room so silent that the air-conditioning unit was giving a concert. I could feel my heart thundering; it was all I paid attention to. I was seated at a testing cubicle with a comfortable, rigid chair and high walls on either side of the desk. Beside and behind me, other students were taking the same test I was, and some were taking different tests for different fields. The not-so-subtle hemispheres in the ceiling watched me intently as I set up my computer workstation and put my test-issued pencils and scratch paper to the side. If I turned my head more than ninety degrees in either direction, the test would be over, and I would be sent home. As the noise-canceling headset descended on my ears, I felt the familiar rush of silence crashing into my mind.

Only six months before I put on that headset, I knew MCAT stood for "Medical College Admission Test." Beyond that, I knew nothing, but suspected that this fabled test, which I had heard about since high school, would be a pretty big challenge.

I was right.

The old MCAT

2014 was the last year in which the MCAT adhered to the "old format" which had existed since 1992 and consisted of four main sections: Physical Sciences, Verbal Reasoning, Biological Sciences, and Writing Sample. Except for the Writing Sample, all sections are still on today's MCAT under different names.

It is important to mention that the MCAT is, was, and will always be passage-based. You will read a page-long passage about a specific topic and then be asked a handful (5-7) of questions regarding the material covered in the passage. A few may ask you to regurgitate some knowledge of the relevant discipline, but most will require you to quickly process and draw conclusions from the information presented in the reading. Some of the questions on the MCAT are discrete, better referred to as "stand-alone." You will learn to love or hate these questions, which are always preceded by the text "Questions X through Y are NOT related to a passage."

The Physical Sciences and Biological Sciences sections covered the pre-med's bread-and-butter: physics, general chemistry, biology, and organic chemistry. To have a firm grounding in all four of these sections, it was recommended to take two semesters of Biophysics, two semesters of General Chemistry, two semesters of Organic Chemistry, and various biology courses such as Cell & Molecular Biology, Zoology, Animal Physiology, and Biochemistry.

The Verbal Reasoning section was...different. Entirely passage-based, this section did not require you to have any prior knowledge of what was discussed in the passages presented to you, but DID expect you to be able to read the passage, understand it, and answer questions related to it. Not only were you expected to process the information presented to you, but you also had to evaluate the possible bias of the author and what the same author might say in new situations. Such questions required careful analysis, patient reflection, and no small degree of personal interpretation; it was not uncommon to have students blatantly disagreeing with the interpretations made by the test designers. I personally was guilty of it, along with every classmate I asked. Regardless, Verbal Reasoning was by far my favorite section of the three, and it was also my best section.

A few years before I took the test, the Writing Sample section was omitted and replaced with a Trial Section. This section was not scored, and consisted of forty-five minutes worth of questions covering material on the new "MR5" MCAT, to be implemented in 2015.

After receiving enough information from students taking the Trial Section, the Association of American Medical Colleges (AAMC) released the MR5 MCAT. This test will be your proving ground.

The new MCAT

The MCAT you will be taking, the MR5 version implemented in 2015, was created in response to several surveys conducted by the AAMC in which medical school faculty were asked what subjects they felt were essential for the doctors of the future. The responses, which emphasized the old curriculum, also cried out for medical students with a better grounding in two major fields: biochemistry and the social sciences.

The implementation of an MCAT with an emphasis on biochemistry should come as no surprise to us. After all, one of the cornerstones of a physician's knowledge is a firm grounding in the chemistry of life. What should come as a surprise is that it wasn't emphasized in the first place. What kind of doctor doesn't know what an amino acid is, but can talk your ears off about the industrial extraction of organic compounds? While some (including myself) suspect that the AAMC had been sneaking more biochemistry into the MCAT even before this change, the emphasis of this essential topic is both necessary and prudent.

It may surprise you to hear that the AAMC also decided to put an emphasis on the social sciences of psychology and sociology, but this can also be explained with good logic. Physicians have always been community leaders, not just medical experts, and it is reasonable to expect those who want to pursue medical school to have a firm grounding in the science of society, and of feeling, and of thought. Knowledge of these fields will empower a physician to promote the positive kind of change we need in our communities to keep the sick from ever getting sick in the first place. That is the best medicine anyone could ask for. In addition, knowledge of the social sciences will enable a physician to deduce the possible psychological issues underlying physical symptoms, as recent studies have confirmed a correlation between these previously disparate entities of medicine.

There are four sections of your MCAT, and the total exam time has been increased from 4.5 hours to a whopping 7.5. With a total of 230 questions (up from 144), the MR5 hopes that a longer, tougher exam will allow for better representation of your potential to succeed in medical school, for several reasons.

First, your boards will be six to eight hours in length. Those are the exams you have to take to become a physician that is licensed to practice medicine in the United States. You also have to re-take your boards every ten years that you are a practicing physician to ensure you are still medically qualified. Whether or not pre-meds should have to take such a long exam so early in their studies, however, is up for debate.

Second, more questions mean more allowable mistakes. My MCAT's scoring system consisted of a maximum of fifteen points allotted to each section, resulting in a total possible score of 45. Most got around a thirty, but *no one* got a 45. It was not nearly as common as getting, say, a 36 on the ACT, and the reason was that the scoring system was weighted. If, for instance, you received ten points on Verbal Reasoning, then you probably missed ten questions or so. However, if you got a thirteen, then you missed two. Obviously, the score was way out of whack.

AAMC's response? Give everybody more points. Now, the MR5 has a score system exceeding even the pre-law LSAT in quantity: you now get up to 132 points for each of the four sections, resulting in a total of 528 possible points!

Tyler L. Scaff

The MCAT's sections

Now, for a quick run-down of the MCAT's anatomy: First is the Biological & Biochemical Foundations of Living Systems Section Test. Long name, but then, what administration doesn't love changing woefully succinct names like "Biological Sciences" to wonderfully ponderous ones? Next, you will face the Chemical & Physical Foundations of Biological Systems Section Test (another re-naming, this one being Physical Sciences). Third in line is the brand-new Psychological, Social & Biological Foundations of Behavior Section Test, and fourth and final is the Critical Analysis & Reasoning Skills Section Test (i.e. Verbal Reasoning). Averaging ninety minutes and sixty-five questions each, these four sections are guaranteed to keep your nails chewed off for the entirety of junior year.

In any case, I am not qualified to write a full reference text for everything you may cover on the MCAT. As such, I have written this chapter merely to serve as an introduction to what you will face. I will tell you what worked for me and my colleagues; choose the path that you think is best for you, or forge your own.

128

Studying on a budget

My family has never had a lot of money. My mother worked as an insurance adjuster, and my father stayed home to raise me and my older sister. We were comfortable, and occasionally saved up enough for a two-week vacation to the Outer Banks. My sister went to college on a full-ride, and I had my bills paid by the Gatton Academy for two years.

When the economy tanked, the vacation and several other frills had to go. My father got a job as a bus driver, but that was not enough to stifle the loans I had accrued in college, or the fact that my mother had reached her raise limit. In a time of inflation, my parents were on a fixed income, and my job paid very little. So when the MCAT came along, I knew I was going to have to study on a budget.

The primary four vendors of MCAT study materials are Kaplan, Examkrackers, Princeton, and AAMC. Some students tried to study for the MCAT using nothing but their old textbooks, but I have never heard of that going well for them. The textbooks we are used to reading are raw sources of information, but the MCAT is a thinking test. It's not just *what* you're studying; it's *how* you apply it. Moreover, your textbooks may cover reams of information that the MCAT will not, and may omit details that the AAMC considers essential. How frustrating it is to stay up all night studying for a test, only to realize you studied all the wrong stuff!

Kaplan is the most expensive option, and perhaps the most popular. A well-established name in graduate exam studies, Kaplan offers courses for the LSAT, DAT, GRE, MCAT, and many other standardized tests. Several physicians I have shadowed, along with many of my colleagues, can attest to Kaplan's effectiveness and reliability in raising your score. They offer structured classes, live lectures, practice tests and questions galore. The downside? You will have to drop around $2000 to get the cheapest package. That was not an option for me. However, if you can afford it, then look at it as an investment in your future; after all, you'll be around $200,000 in debt after graduating medical school, so what's $2000 now?

Examkrackers has a similar reputation to Kaplan, and the cost for their book-based course is a paltry $200. You will not get the same level of instruction that Kaplan offers, since live lectures and online work are not the focus of the course, but Examkrackers has a reputation rivaling even that of Kaplan. Remember, it costs over $200 to register for *a single* MCAT test day. Medical school is expensive even before it's expensive.

The Princeton Review is essentially the same as Kaplan in quality, reputation, and cost (about $2300). There is a certain feeling of security in making such an investment that may prove invaluable on test day: The knowledge that you have paid the most to get the best will instill in you a sense of confidence, something that runs in short supply when faced with the MCAT.

All of the above systems, along with the ones you find on your own, will highly recommend that you make use of the AAMC's official practice materials. The AAMC offers you one free practice MCAT, and many more for $35 a pop. This was the resource of which I and my fellow students made the most use. Of all the test prep resources out there, the AAMC is the most qualified to show you what the AAMC will test you on. I and several of my friends bought the official test prep book that they offer, which contains passages and full-length paper practice tests, in addition to another resource they offer which consists of three-hour-long practice tests over specific disciplines (e.g. Physics or General Chemistry), just in case you don't have enough to work on.

As you descend farther into the madness that is MCAT studying, you will begin to discern subtle differences in the questions provided by critically acclaimed test prep companies, such as Kaplan, and those provided by the AAMC itself. Some from unofficial sources will be less clear as to what they are asking, or will cover material closely related to what the AAMC has listed as possible material, but not close enough to be something you may actually see. **The AAMC has outlined all of the material the MCAT covers in a document on their website.** I would encourage you to visit their website and read that document carefully before you begin studying.

Your college may offer a pre-professional exam preparation course, and some offer MCAT-specific courses. When I studied for the exam, I took a local $200 preparation course that met every Saturday for an average of four hours. It served as a good refresher, and an inexpensive way to get access to around ten official practice tests. Consider your institution when looking for ways to study; ask around and see what opportunities may be just down the road.

The MCAT is an incredible challenge, and it is likely to be the largest obstacle standing between you and medical school. However, do not allow the test to intimidate you; stick to your study schedule, take time to de-stress, and know that when the time comes, you *will* be ready to face it.

Applying to Medical School

You have to pay to pay to apply to pay to apply to apply to medical school. Alternatively, you could apply to *not* pay to *not* pay to apply to *not* pay to apply to apply to medical school, but that requires that you apply to *not* pay.

What you have just read is the summary of this chapter, and no, I did not make a mistake. Let me break the application process down for you as it currently exists:

Pay $200 to take the MCAT (OR apply for fee waiver)

Pay $36 per medical school application (OR apply for fee waiver)

Apply with American Medical College Application Service (AMCAS)

Pay $50-$200 for secondary application (OR apply for fee waivers)

Fill out one unique secondary application per medical school

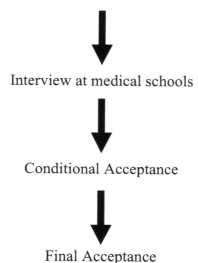

Interview at medical schools

Conditional Acceptance

Final Acceptance

     Medical school is expensive before it's expensive, not just in terms of money but also in terms of time. Expect to spend the majority of your second junior semester dealing with this complicated process of applications and tests.

The big test

There is one big reason why many people choose not to be doctors: It is a long, hard road, and it includes the formidable MCAT, a test so intimidating that travelers huddled around campfires fear to speak its name. The previous chapter covered the MCAT in detail; remember, you *can* handle it. It will not be a pleasant experience, but you will make it through.

As mentioned in the previous chapter, the MCAT costs $200 *per attempt*. As with any part of the AAMC's medical school application process, you can apply for a fee waiver if you are below a certain poverty line. These fee waivers will be effective for both the MCAT registration fee and the AMCAS $36-per-school fees. You will have to apply for secondary application fee waivers individually.

AMCAS

Once your wallet is two hundred dollars lighter, and you are satisfied with your MCAT score, you will apply to medical school using AMCAS. AMCAS is like the "CommonApp" for medical schools; that is, it is a universal application that can be used to apply to any medical school in the United States. Nine wonderful parts comprise this application:

1. Identifying Information – Name, relevant ID numbers, birth, sex.

2. Schools Attended – What high school you went to, what colleges you have attended, and whether or not you previously matriculated to medical school.

3. Biographic Information – Address, relatives, military service, language proficiencies, citizenship, minority status.

4. Course Work – A comprehensive list of every course you ever took in college. By far, this is the most time-consuming section.

5. Work/Activities – A list of fifteen slots where you can describe any job, volunteering opportunity, mission trip, or research endeavor you ever undertook. Fifteen slots may sound like a lot, but you will have to decide what to list and what to leave out.

6. Letters of Evaluation – One letter from your pre-med committee or a letter packet from professors at your

university, along with any other letters of recommendation you wish to include.

7. Medical Schools – A list of what medical schools you choose to apply to. $36 each.

8. Essay(s) – Your personal statement, along with additional essays that are required if you pursue an M.D./Ph.D. program.

9. Standardized Tests – Your score on the MCAT, along with any other standardized graduate exams you have taken (such as the GRE).

The AMCAS application will initially open for data entry only. For the period of one month, you will be able to enter in your information, but not submit the application. The window for submission will then open after that month has elapsed. You will then have to ensure that your MCAT scores and letters of evaluation arrive.

A note on pre-med committees: A pre-med committee is a group of three professors chosen from a list of those at your school that are committee-eligible. If your university has this system (and most universities do), you can go online to see who you can select for your committee. You must select three professors, two of whom are in the sciences. One must be willing to chair the committee, and all must know you pretty well. Near the end of your junior year, you will meet with each committee member individually and be interviewed as if you are in a medical school interview. Then, during the summer, the committee will meet privately and discuss your qualifications to become a doctor.

After they have reached a consensus, they will submit a Letter of Evaluation to AMCAS. *This is not a letter of recommendation.* It is an attempt to objectively analyze your capabilities to become a physician. Remember that this is not an application to a research internship, or summer camp, or even to a job. You are applying to become one of the privileged few who hold lives in their hands every day, and the people who interview you know this. They all take their job of evaluating you with the utmost seriousness; even if the professors evaluating you are your friends, they are still professionals first and will do their best to be objective. AMCAS as a whole is designed to put you under the most uncomfortable light possible and watch you squirm under pressure, but it is designed that way to weed out those who are going into this field for the wrong reasons.

Submit your application on the first day that the submission window opens. The importance of this cannot be overstated. Submitting your application right on time will automatically put you a step ahead of the competition, and set you up for interviews that fall instead of the following spring. Medical school classes fill up on a first-come, first-considered basis. The more on the ball you are, the more likely you will get in. I submitted my application three hours after the submission window opened, and my first interview was in late August of that same year. It was truly a relief to be accepted into medical school before my fall semester had elapsed. Remember, you do not have to have your MCAT scores or letters of evaluation in before you submit the application. AMCAS will still process your application while waiting on those things to arrive. Once all the pieces are assembled, your application will be processed for a couple of weeks and then be marked "complete". Once that has happened, your application will be visible to the medical schools to which you have chosen to apply.

Secondary applications

Should you pique the interest of a school (or if they just want more of your money), you will be sent a secondary application soon after your AMCAS application is complete. Secondary applications, or "secondaries" for short, are smaller applications that are unique to each medical school. They usually contain a page's worth of biographical information, a couple of pages of short-answer questions ("What careers other than medicine interest you?"), and one or two page-long essays. Secondaries take a deceptively long period of time to complete, so get started on them as soon as they arrive in your inbox. Then, you will pay anywhere from $50 to $200 to submit this secondary application. (So the minimum total money that you need to apply to a single medical school is $200 + $36 + $50 = $286.)

Now, the waiting game begins. You have submitted your primary and secondary applications to your dream medical school, and they will look over your application and decide if they like what they see. If they are not sure, or if you applied late, you may receive a notification that you have been placed on an interview waitlist. That means that when someone comes in and flubs their interview, you will get to take their place if you are first on the list.

If, however, your application was turned in on time, and looks decent, you may get an interview in the fall semester of your senior year. You will receive an email in your inbox notifying you of this invitation to interview, and you will have only a few days to a week to select an interview time. NOTE: Sometimes the email is lost! I have had friends who were invited to interview but never received the email, even after checking their spam folder. If you are waiting to hear from the medical school for more than a

month, give their admissions office a call to check in with
them.

The interview

So here you are, finally interviewing at a medical school. This means that the medical school has decided that your academic history, MCAT scores, and overall personality as it was depicted in the application make you a qualified candidate for medical school. Be proud of this accomplishment, because the medical school believes you would be a good doctor on paper. The interview, however, is designed to get to know you as a person. They want to know that you are a professional, dedicated, personable, and intelligent student who would excel in the rigorous atmosphere of medical school.

From this, I have devised a list of Dos and Don'ts for interviewing at a medical school.

✓ **Do:** *Tell the interviewer why you want to be a doctor.* Think about this question beforehand because it is a lot harder to answer than you might think. By far, it is the question that interviewers ask most often.

✓ **Do:** *Have a mock interview or two with pre-medical professors.* They have prepared young doctors for years and are extremely qualified to give you advice.

✓ **Do:** *Dress the part.* Men, get a two-button suit and tie, and polish up your wingtip shoes. Comb your hair and get a shave. Ladies, get a pantsuit or conservative business dress. Pull back your hair into a professional-looking ponytail or bun so it does not get in your face. Don't overdo it on makeup, wear small earrings if any, and don't wear very high heels. (You may be taking a tour of the medical school on interview day.) Regardless of what sex you are, remember that the key to any interview is to dress like you have already got the job. No, don't wear a lab coat or stethoscope, but look as professional as a physician is expected to look. Get your outfit dry-cleaned before the interview.

✓ **Do:** *Show up fifteen minutes early for the interview; no more, no less.* If you have to get up at 5:00 AM to beat traffic, then do it. It is acceptable to arrive early and then kill some time before heading to the interview building, but it is unacceptable to be late.

✓ **Do:** *Come up with good questions you want to ask the interviewer about the medical school.* At the end of many interviews, you will be asked if you have any questions. Don't ask about the food or the cost of living or anything you could find in a pamphlet, because you will just be wasting the interviewer's time. Do ask about programs the medical school offers, possibilities for research, or a recent accreditation, grant, or award that the medical school received. Show that you have a strong interest in this particular medical school, and that you will show up next year raring to get involved.

X Don't: *Wear the colors of the school at which you are interviewing.* That will be viewed as a tacky brownnosing maneuver, and will not be looked upon favorably. Wear dark, professional hues. On interview day, I wore a navy blue pinstripe suit with a diagonally striped red-and-black tie and a white collared shirt, with wingtip shoes. Be conservative, not creative.

X Don't: *Respond with clichés.* Your interviewers have heard it all before. Don't tell them that you want to be a doctor just so you can save lives and help people, because that is what everyone will say. Come up with answers that are unique to *you* and *your* life.

X Don't: *Rely on anecdotes to tell your story.* Medical schools do not accept people who want to become doctors just because their aunt had a heart attack last year and they wish they could have helped them. That may have served as a catalytic event, galvanizing you on the path to medicine, but you should want to become a doctor because *it is just who you are.* You should like the science, the challenge, the human body as a machine, and the idea of serving your fellow man every day. You should also have had several positive shadowing experiences that you cannot wait to tell the interviewer about. Finally, you should imply that if you do not make it this cycle, you will try again and again, year after year, until you get a shot at becoming a physician. Don't be annoying about it, but don't be afraid to show your dedication to this career field. It is a delicate balance.

X **Don't:** *Talk about your academics exclusively.* Many medical school interviewees seem to feel that the interview is just another chance for you to flaunt your impressive MCAT score or GPA, or discuss how sad you were when you got a B in first-year chemistry. The medical school has heard enough about your academics from the application. Use the interview as an opportunity to share more about yourself, and what kind of person you are outside the academic world. Talk about your extracurricular activities, your research, your shadowing experiences, or your personal experiences in medicine. Discuss how these experiences made you want to be a doctor, and made you qualified to be a medical student. Sell yourself on the home front.

X **Don't:** *Say you want to become a doctor for the money.* Just don't.

X **Don't:** *Imbibe the night before going to the interview.* I would recommend you spend the night before reviewing some questions that may be asked and getting a good night's sleep, rather than relaxing with a cold one. Even if you have a high tolerance, it's just not worth the risk of a hangover.

The competition

Before discussing acceptance, I must warn you of a fundamental truth of applying to medical school: The competition you have in this race consists almost entirely of the exception. Were you one of the students who constantly messed up the grading curve with your high test scores? Have you volunteered at your local clinic since middle school? Do you look back on your high school accomplishments and smile as you think about how far ahead you are of those your age?

That's great, but all your other competitors are precisely in the same boat. Some are in better boats.

In the world of medical school applications, there is a whole new average, and you and I are smack-dab in the middle. Zoom in on the right side of the college bell curve, and you'll find another bell curve made up of the most learned people ever to have existed on the planet. Take pride in knowing you are somewhere on there, and now let that pride sink.

Medical schools will not bat an eye at your solid 3.80 GPA, nor will the jaws of the admissions committees hit the floor when they see how dedicated you are to community service. There are applicants who have taught English in Korea for two years while attending college full-time (I know one). In their personal statements, some will discuss the most recent suicide they prevented, or baby they delivered, or the fact that their parent is Chief of Chief Resident Chiefs at Johns Hopkins. Some have photographic memories, know four languages, scored perfectly on every standardized test they ever took, play instruments you've never even heard of, volunteered in Uganda, rub shoulders with the elite, and have enough money to sink a coal barge. Some have had private tutors for the MCAT since high school and their personal statement is currently undergoing another revision by an English professor at Yale. These are the ones who might raise eyebrows on interview day, and they are your competitors.

But take heart. Most medical school applicants are in our boat, so it is our goal to stand out from the competition in the best ways available to us. That takes work, self-discipline, and confidence in yourself, and if you use your time in college wisely, you **will** get into a medical school. It may not be Weill Cornell Medical College, but it will be a medical school, and that is an important thing to understand. Your patients will rarely care which medical school you attended, as long as you are a good doctor with your heart in the right place. When your confidence is hurt in watching your classmates surpass you, academically or otherwise, remember that you are still on the route to medicine, and being "number one" is no longer relevant to your pursuits. Take this to heart, and your application process will be far less stressful than you think it might be.

Acceptance

Finally, the time comes to wait for admission notifications. Weeks will pass and seem like months, but eventually you will receive an email or physical letter from the medical school offering you a seat in their class. Alternatively, you could get declined or waitlisted, much like in the college admissions process. One school to which I applied had a system that gave you a phone call from your interviewer if you were accepted, an email if you were waitlisted, or a letter if you were declined. Ultimately, I called them and learned that I was accepted. I then received an email *and* a physical letter notifying me of my acceptance…I'm not quite sure what I was supposed to take away from receiving all three.

When offered a seat, you have the option to conditionally accept the seat or decline it. Conditional acceptance means you can hold that seat and still hold other seats, should you be offered them, at other medical schools. You only have a couple of weeks to decide on the conditional acceptance, so act fast. If you fail to send a reply within that time, you run the risk of them offering your seat to someone else.

After you have conditionally accepted the seat, you are officially on the road to becoming a doctor. As long as your background check clears and you maintain your academic standing in college (i.e., successfully graduate), you will be offered final acceptance the spring before you are scheduled to matriculate. Final acceptance is, truly, the final acceptance decision you have to make. You can have multiple conditional acceptances, but when the time comes, you can only attend one medical school, and that is where you will stay for the next four years. **Transfers or gap years**

in medical school are extremely rare; you almost always have to stay at the same school for all four years to become a physician.

Medical schools have an interesting love-hate relationship with their applicants. They begin by putting you, the applicant, under an extremely uncomfortable spotlight for four years, forcing you to work your keister off to show them you can handle it. Then, when you are accepted, you are welcomed into the fold. All of a sudden, the medical school starts trying to sell itself to you! Administrators will email you, call you, and invite you to seminar after seminar. Eagerly they will show you all that their medical school has to offer, and when you choose to attend that school, you are even more of an asset to them. Medical schools must choose their classes carefully, since there are no do-overs; any failure or dropout leaves a gaping hole in the class that cannot be filled (remember: no transfer students).

So when you do attend medical school, know that you will become part of a community that is tighter than any group in college. You will have a strong support system of administrators, counselors, fellow students, and professional physicians, all of whom want to see you succeed. The application process is difficult, but the rewards, in my opinion, are well worth it.

A Final Word

Most medical schools in America have adopted a relatively new tradition that starts your first year off with a bang, or rather, a coat.

The White Coat Ceremony (WCC) is an event in which you and your fellow first-year (M1) medical students are presented with waist-length white coats to affirm your commitment to medicine. Usually, the presentation of the coat is either preceded or followed by a reading of a medical oath, commonly the Hippocratic Oath.

The original version of the Hippocratic Oath, while rather outdated, nonetheless captures the spirit of being a physician. The translation of the original Oath according to the National Institutes of Health (NIH) reads as follows:

I swear by Apollo the physician, and Asclepius, and Hygieia and Panacea and all the gods and goddesses as my witnesses, that, according to my ability and judgement, I will keep this Oath and this contract:

To hold him who taught me this art equally dear to me as my parents, to be a partner in life with him, and to fulfill his needs when required; to look upon his offspring as equals to my own siblings, and to teach them this art, if they shall wish to learn it, without fee or contract; and that by the set rules, lectures, and every other mode of instruction, I will impart a knowledge of the art to my own sons, and those of my teachers, and to students bound by this contract and having sworn this Oath to the law of medicine, but to no others.

I will use those dietary regimens which will benefit my patients according to my greatest ability and judgement, and I will do no harm or injustice to them.

I will not give a lethal drug to anyone if I am asked, nor will I advise such a plan; and similarly I will not give a woman a pessary [intravaginal device] *to cause an abortion.*

In purity and according to divine law will I carry out my life and my art.

I will not use the knife [perform surgery], *even upon those suffering from stones, but I will leave this to those who are trained in this craft.*

Into whatever homes I go, I will enter them for the benefit of the sick, avoiding any voluntary act of impropriety or corruption, including the seduction of women or men, whether they are free men or slaves.

Whatever I see or hear in the lives of my patients, whether in connection with my professional practice or not, which ought not to be spoken of outside, I will keep secret, as considering all such things to be private.

So long as I maintain this Oath faithfully and without corruption, may it be granted to me to partake of life fully and the practice of my art, gaining the respect of all men for all time. However, should I transgress this Oath and violate it, may the opposite be my fate.[2]

---

[2] North, M. (2002). Greek Medicine - National Institutes of Health. Retrieved March 16, 2015.

Most medical schools modify the original Hippocratic Oath to make it more relevant to today's medical environment; however, some choose to keep the original. Some medical schools permit students to write their own vows and recite them during the White Coat Ceremony, whereas still others do not take vows at all.

Affirming an oath is a dated practice in and of itself, yet it is my belief that taking a vow of service adds a much-needed spiritual component to the practice of medicine. Too often on this hard road will you find yourself bogged down by the bureaucracy of patient care, the minutiae of grades, and the semantics of your résumé. Never forget that medicine is a timeless and noble profession, and choosing to pursue a career in it is choosing to serve your fellow man. It is a field that is constantly evolving; thus, even after you complete your residency you will still be a student of the craft.

Ultimately, as a doctor, you will be a leader of qualified medical professionals in your specialty of choice. As a medical student, you will be a student of what I believe is the most exciting and gratifying career ever to exist. As a pre-med, you will be taking baby steps to a bright future. Keep your eyes on the goal, and avoid the temptation to stray. Let your passion for service be the fire that drives your train forward, accelerating relentlessly through college, through medical school, through internship, through residency and beyond into your career.

The path to medicine begins with college, and it is rife with obstacles that can easily be labeled as impassable. However, doctors today are testament to the fact that the only true barrier between a determined pre-med and his or her patients is time. All other barricades are demolished by power of will. Develop and protect your determination to be a doctor, and in time you also will don the white coat.

As a graduating pre-med, and a future medical student, I wish you a bright future as a medical professional. I'll see you at rounds.

Acknowledgements

The idea for this book came from a desire to provide you, the reader, with a roadmap for the obstacles you may face as a pre-med college student. I did not have such a resource when I was attempting to navigate this environment, and without the help of my friends and family I certainly would not have gotten to where I am now.

First, the gratitude I have for my family cannot be overstated. My parents have always encouraged me to pursue fields of my own interest; whenever I showed interest in a career path, they helped me explore it further. I was interested in science, so they took me to science museums. I was interested in aviation, so they saved up for a flight lesson. I was interested in medicine, so they connected me with the local Medical Explorers club in my hometown. They never pushed me in a specific direction, but rather let me find my own way. In doing so, my parents taught me to stand on my own, and to have the self-discipline to realize my dreams. I cannot express how much I love and appreciate them.

Second, I want to thank my best friend Logan Eckler for his detailed editing of this book, and for his encouraging me to see it through. He also offered me some valuable advice for self-publishing and getting this book on the market. You've always had my back, and I'll always have yours.

Thirdly, I would like to express my appreciation to all the physicians, professors, and members of the community who have helped me get as far as I have. Dr. Rodney King, Dr. Ken Crawford, and Dr. Wieb van der

Meer comprised my pre-med committee, but countless others have helped me through their instruction, advice, and moral support. I would especially like to thank Dr. Pokey Bowen for the two years of wise counseling he provided me in the Gatton Academy. His desire to listen and offer advice helped me through one of the most difficult times of my life.

I would also like to thank Dr. Luke Murray, who provided a physician's point of view on this book, wrote a foreword, and helped me clarify the things I wished to share with those considering a pre-medical major or concentration in college. He has been an invaluable resource and friend.

Finally, I want to thank you, reader, for considering my advice as you go forward in your medical career. It is a very rewarding feeling to know that my words may help ease the path of some future physicians, and I hope you have found something within this book that you may take with you. Medicine is a hard road, but there will always be those who want to see you succeed. After all, someday you may be their doctor.